Wedding Etiquette

Wedding Etiquette

The Complete Guide to Planning Your Wedding

LIBBY NORMAN

NEW HOLLAND

First published in 2007 by New Holland Publishers (UK) Ltd
London • Cape Town • Sydney • Auckland

10 9 8 7 6 5 4 3 2 1

www.newhollandpublishers.com

Garfield House, 86–88 Edgware Road, London W2 2EA, UK

80 McKenzie Street, Cape Town 8001, South Africa

14 Aquatic Drive, Frenchs Forest, NSW 2086, Australia

218 Lake Road, Northcote, Auckland, New Zealand

ISBN 978 1 84537 688 8

Editorial Director: Jo Hemmings
Editor: Kate Parker
Design concept: Bill Mason
Design: Gülen Shevki-Taylor
Cover design: Ian Hughes, Mousemat Design Ltd
Production: Hema Gohil

Cover reproduction by Pica Digital PTE Ltd, Singapore
Printed and bound in India by Replika Press Pvt. Ltd

Note: The author and publishers have made every effort to ensure that the information
given in this book is safe and accurate, but they cannot accept liability for any
resulting injury or loss or damage to either property or person, whether direct or
consequential and howsoever arising.

CONTENTS

INTRODUCTION

Who said romance was dead? If you've already broken the news, you will have realised from the misty-eyed, champagne-popping reactions that your wedding is a very big deal – not just for you, but for just about everybody you know. And if you haven't let family and friends in on the secret yet, get ready for endless questions about when, where and how you intend to tie that knot.

This is where *Wedding Etiquette* comes in, by showing you how to create the celebration you want and taking the stress out of the planning process. This book does not tell you what you *must* do (after all, weddings are as unique as the people getting married), but it does outline key options and helps you narrow down choices, as well as offering practical guidance on major decisions and small but important details.

Throughout the six chapters, you will find useful information about customs and traditions surrounding marriage. Some you may choose to ignore, but understanding the way things used to be organised is useful knowledge when you're dealing with relatives and friends who don't understand modern wedding etiquette.

There are also Troubleshooting Sections at the end of Chapters One to Five giving solutions to real-life wedding dilemmas, including pacifying offended relatives, marrying someone from a different religious or cultural background and managing difficult wedding guests.

We begin with beginnings: the proposal and engagement. Getting Engaged (page 8) covers who to tell first and how, choosing rings (including how much to spend), and planning an engagement party. There's also guidance on making those initial tentative decisions that create a framework for your day.

First Wedding Plans (page 26) gets down to business, outlining the first essential 'to do' list that will get your show on the road. There's advice on fixing a wedding date and deciding on budgets – including working out who pays. You will also find out how to decide on the best venue for you, tailor your celebration to make it more or less formal and draw up that all-important guest list.

Choosing Your Support Team (page 46) offers the low-down on picking the perfect best man and bridesmaids. There's advice on finding other roles for family and friends plus useful tips on the fine art of delegating. With the support team primed and ready, there's a how-to section on planning (and surviving) stag and hen night parties. And if you don't like that convention, check out the suggestions for alternative pre-wedding parties.

Paperwork & Practicalities (page 64) covers legal announcements and provides sample wordings for newspaper notices and wedding invitations. There's guidance on gift lists, choosing and vetting suppliers, and planning for unexpected extra costs. You will also find out how to change names – and who to inform if you do. The chapter ends with a useful at-a-glance wedding planner, giving essential timings in the run up to your marriage.

The Big Day (page 88) takes you through everything from arriving on time to seating plans at the ceremony and reception. There's guidance on the service itself, plus checklists for managing still and video photography, entertaining junior guests and ensuring the speeches and toasts run smoothly. You will also learn how to stage-manage the perfect first dance and get the party going. And since all good things come to an end, the chapter concludes with tips for getting die-hard party animals to leave.

The Honeymoon & After (page 110) has pointers for planning your dream holiday – whatever your budget – and then managing the return to real life. There's a checklist to help you tie up final loose ends from the wedding, plus a special section on creating the perfect thank-you note.

Don't forget to check out the Useful Sources section (from page 120), listing who to contact for everything from hen night planning to gift lists.

However you choose to design your wedding – quiet register office ceremony or champagne party for 300 – enjoy the celebration. After all, this is your big day!

CHAPTER 1

GETTING ENGAGED

*This is it — you're going to get married and it's
going to be the perfect wedding day...
But once you climb off cloud nine,
reality sets in. You've got an awful lot of
organisation to do. Not only have you got to
break the news to all and sundry, but you've
also got to choose rings, set dates and
decide where on earth to get married.
Then there's the whole business of
engagement parties, wedding planning and
managing other people's expectations.
This first chapter gives you a step-by-step
guide to being engaged — starting with passing
on the good news and ending with a checklist
guide to making the first tentative outline for
your wedding day.*

SPREADING THE NEWS

Deciding to get married is a milestone event so this is a hot piece of news you will want to share. But your feelings of joy might not be shared by family and friends if you get the timing of the announcement wrong, allow someone close to you to hear the news second hand or – worst of all gaffes – forget to tell someone important altogether. The best way to ensure that everyone has a positive response is to get together as a couple and do some strategic planning.

DID YOU KNOW...? AGE OF CONSENT

In England, Wales and the Republic of Ireland, under-18s still need to get written permission from a parent or guardian before they can get married. In some cases, if this permission is refused, the couple can apply to court. In Scotland – home of the famous elopement town of Gretna Green – anyone aged 16 or above is allowed to plight their troth. Northern Ireland won't allow couples to marry even with parental consent until they are 17.

✧ TELLING YOUR FAMILY

The news may not come as a surprise. You may even have discussed plans or hinted at what's to come. But still the announcement of an engagement is a chance for those closest to you to crack open the champagne and drink to your future happiness.

Parents

Traditionally, the father of the bride's permission was sought first, sometimes even before the formal proposal to the bride. This convention, dating back to an era when most unmarried women lived with their family, gave parents or guardians the chance to ask the man searching questions about his 'prospects' and ensure that he was good marriage material.

Some grooms-to-be still like to adhere to the old convention of approaching the bride's father formally (although it's always a good idea to wait until she's said yes!), but in most cases you will want to break the news to both sets of parents at around the same time. Do this in person if you can, although a phone call is perfectly acceptable if the news can't wait or if parents live some distance away.

If parents are divorced, one parent is going to hear before the other one, but you can still make this as fair as possible by ringing them in quick succession. Remember to be inclusive and also discuss the good news with their current partners.

CONFERENCE CALLING

If you can't break the news in person, or can't wait to tell, the easiest way to let both sets of parents in on the secret at the same time is to each use a mobile phone and make the calls home simultaneously. This also gives you the chance to swap handsets and speak to your future in-laws.

Siblings

Brothers and sisters are often told at the earliest stage – even before parents if you are particularly close and just can't suppress your excitement. If they do hear first, remember to swear them to secrecy. If you are closer to one sibling and they get the scoop, just remember to fill your other siblings in on all the details as soon as you can. Never let them hear it from your parents or another family member or they will justifiably feel side-lined.

Other Relatives

If one thing reveals the importance of a wedding, it's the reaction of relatives to the news of an engagement. You may find that aunts and uncles you barely see from one wedding to the next christening suddenly take a deep personal interest in your affairs. It is important to be sensitive about this, even if you don't feel particularly close to them. Remember that they may hold cherished memories of you as an adorable curly-haired toddler and feel this gives them a 'stake' in your future happiness. Get guidance from your parents on the best approach but you should almost certainly call or write a personal note to let them know you are engaged before the formal invitations are sent. The same goes for godparents – they kindly agreed to be your moral guardians some time in the dim and distant past, so it's only fair to let them know about such a key event in your life.

True life stories: Family feuds

When Simon and Elaine got engaged they thought they were doing things by the book, but because there was a gap of just a few months between their engagement and wedding they neglected to tell all their relatives the news personally. One aunt and uncle, who knew nothing of the engagement until they received the gold-embossed invitation, refused point-blank to come to the wedding. It took several pleading phone calls and a personal visit by the couple before they could be persuaded. 'It just hadn't occurred to us that they could take offence when we were inviting them to such a happy event,' says Simon. 'The mistake we made was treating them like the other guests when they thought that as family they had a right to special treatment.'

DID YOU KNOW...? PROMISES, PROMISES

Although engagements have no legal status today, in Victorian times once a woman said 'yes' it was considered a contract. This meant that if the man broke off the engagement he could be sued for breach of promise. She, on the other hand, could walk away without any financial penalty or stain on her reputation.

✧ TELLING FRIENDS AND COLLEAGUES
Friends

Your circle of friends plays a vital role in planning the big day – some of them may have been instrumental in your first meeting. They will want to share your news and usually find out when the parties start. Phone calls and emails will spread the news fast, but you can meet close friends at a bar or pub to break the news personally (allowing them to buy you a celebratory drink). Remember to be circumspect about your wedding plans – especially after an evening of toasts – so that you don't end up with three nominees for best man or an unmanageable bevy of bridesmaids. The stag or hen night is almost more of an event in some quarters – again be careful not to run away with wild plans until you've worked out the details and likely cost implications and discussed them with your partner.

Colleagues and employer

How you share the excitement with work colleagues depends both on the depth of your friendship and the general workplace atmosphere. Pub, cream cakes all round or lunchtime sorties to the travel agent/bridal shop can all work. In the case of your employer, it is important to break the news gently and with a degree of formality. Announcing an impending marriage may be your private business, but in their eyes it also means mornings off (dress and suit fittings), daydreams ('shall I go for Amsterdam or Zagreb for the stag/hen night?') and a whole host of phone calls and emails to sort out mini crises in the run up to the big day. Go to see your

---

MEMO TO SELF: ACTION PLAN FOR KEEPING BOSS ON SIDE

1 Tell him/her you will try not to let this affect your work (do this before you ask for any favours).

2 If you want extra holiday give as much advance notice as possible. Volunteer to take it off next year's entitlement or as unpaid leave.

3 If you have to take time off for appointments, ask permission in advance. Offer to make up the time missed from work.

4 Play fair with phone calls/emails during office hours.

5 Ensure that you spend at least some time each day talking about subjects not related to your wedding or honeymoon.

6 Don't let minor problems (e.g. can't find right shade of yellow napkins) take over your life. That way your boss will cut you some slack if major ones (e.g. travel firm disappears with honeymoon deposit) do happen.

boss in person if you can. That way you have shown respect for them and for your working relationship. You may be asking a lot of favours in the months to come, so it helps if you get them on your side.

True life stories: Popping the question

If you secretly wish you had experienced the excitement of bended knee and beautifully wrapped jewellery box, then it's worth remembering that romantic gestures sometimes look better on the big screen than in real life. While there is no 'right way' to pop the question, it is definitely possible to get it wrong. Here are two ideas that sounded great... on paper. (Both proposals were, by the way, accepted.)

It happened in Paris

The Eurostar tickets were booked, the restaurant 'à deux' had been carefully selected. What could possibly go wrong? The venue for popping the question was, of course, an iconic one. As Peter plucked up his courage and checked on the ring in his pocket he guided Sarah through the streets of Paris to their destination. When they arrived at the Eiffel Tower he realised immediately there had been a terrible flaw in his plan. The very last lift of the day was ascending the building and the tower was firmly 'fermé'. His proposal was made at the bottom.

Love NY style

A whirlwind shopping trip was bound to touch Bijal's heart, but Steve was planning an even bigger surprise in New York. After a hard day's shopping, he suggested a spontaneous trip up the Empire State Building. This seemed less enticing after they had queued for well over an hour. Finally, they reached the viewing deck where Steve did his best to find a quiet corner. Unfortunately, the large group of Japanese tourists sharing their space not only had their cameras ready, but found the whole sight irresistible. The proposal was made in the glare of flashbulbs and to the sound of polite applause.

FORMAL NEWSPAPER ANNOUNCEMENTS

You don't have to announce your marriage plans in a local or national newspaper, especially since your friends may not be avid readers of the Personals column, but this is a tradition that your parents may want to uphold. After all, it gives them a chance to spread the good news to old friends and colleagues they have lost touch with and sets the seal on an important family rite of passage. The old rule of thumb was that the bride's parents paid for announcements in the national press and the groom's paid for local press announcements. Of course, you may want to avoid all arguments (including the nature of the wording) by paying for the announcement yourself. For ideas on wording traditional and contemporary engagement announcements see page 66.

CHOOSING RINGS

'Bling, bling' or 'understated elegance' is the big decision for rings. And unless you've already spent months deciding on the style and cut of jewel or shape of wedding band, you may feel slightly overawed by the prospect of choosing something 'for life'. It is tricky for the chooser and even harder for the recipient, which is why so many couples go shopping together. Here are some guidelines for both sides.

✧ ENGAGEMENT RING
Tips for the giver:

The old dictum about the engagement ring was that it should cost around two months' salary. This is an outdated idea so don't feel you have to take out a second mortgage or make a bold statement. In truth, a smaller and less ostentatious ring is more practical, since this is a piece of jewellery designed to be worn every day.

If you have a piece of family (estate) jewellery that you would like to use as an engagement ring this can be a lovely tradition – but only if your partner likes the idea. For some brides-to-be, wearing something that originally belonged to another fiancée is off-putting, even bad luck. Or she may not like the stone or the setting. You can change the setting (though this is expensive), but if the gem is not to her taste, it is better to think again.

Don't shop for the ring alone unless you are confident of your partner's taste. You need to know if she prefers white or yellow gold, whether her style is traditional or contemporary and the sort of stone she would like. A close female friend or sibling should be able to guide you on this.

Tips for the receiver:

It can be tricky to point your partner in the right direction on rings, particularly if you are not entirely sure of the amount he has decided to spend. If you can discuss the style of ring you like – physically pointing out examples – then that gives a useful steer.

Offer to go shopping together. He may be under the illusion that you want to be surprised and that it isn't 'romantic' unless you open a mystery box. If you dread the thought of a sight-unseen ring – particularly since this is a piece of jewellery you will be expected to wear all the time – then tell him.

If you do go shopping together, point out rings you like at a variety of different price points. That way you have ensured you are not forcing a budget-busting option onto your partner.

Check he likes the ring too. A small point maybe, but it is his gift to you and carries far more importance than anything else he will ever buy for you.

✧ CHOOSING DIAMONDS

Diamonds are by far the most popular choice for engagement rings because of the hardness of the stone and its symbolic value: it's said to represent lasting love. The three 'C's are what determine its value.

- **Cut** The way a diamond is cut is what gives it sparkle; the more skilfully this is done the more 'bling' you get. Modern diamonds tend to look sparklier than vintage pieces because they are usually cut by laser rather than hand, which means they have more light-reflecting facets.

- **Clarity** The value of a diamond is largely determined by its flawlessness since most stones have tiny impurities that affect the colour. Don't expect to spot these with the naked eye; it may take a jeweller looking at the stone through a magnifying glass with ten-time magnification to spot them.
- **Carat** This is the weight of the diamond. Larger stones are more valuable not only because they are larger, but because of their rarity. A one-carat diamond weighs a fifth of a gram. Size isn't everything though – you may find a smaller diamond costs more than a larger one because it has better clarity.

Other gems

It isn't essential to buy a diamond and many couples opt for a different stone – not least because you may get more for your money and some gems are actually rarer than diamonds. Each stone is said to symbolise a virtue. Here are other options with their popular meanings.

- **Emerald** Leaf to rich green, symbolising hope
- **Ruby** Pale to deep red, symbolising contentment
- **Sapphire** Bright to dark blue, symbolising balance
- **Garnet** Rich red to orange-brown, symbolising truth
- **Topaz** Yellow-gold to tawny brown, symbolising faithfulness
- **Opal** Usually white-grey and opalescent, symbolising love

✧ WEDDING RINGS

While engagement rings can be showstoppers, the rings you will swap on your wedding day are generally simple bands made of white or yellow gold or platinum. It is a good idea to choose the bands from the same jeweller at the same time so they match. You may also want to have the rings engraved. Superstition says you shouldn't buy your engagement ring and wedding bands at the same time, although it makes sense to check the two work well together by trying them on your finger.

RING BUYER'S CHECKLIST

1 Go to a reputable jeweller. Get recommendations from friends and family or look for a member of a national society, such as The British Jewellers' Association.

2 Ask lots of questions before you make your choice. Get the jeweller to show you a variety of stones so you can make a comparison. Also ask them to explain why one is more valuable than another.

3 Make it clear this is an engagement ring to be worn daily and not a dress ring to be worn occasionally. Ask them if the ring is suitable for daily wear and remember that a raised setting might catch on clothing – a bad idea if you do hands-on work.

4 Get the ring altered to fit when you buy it. Jewellers will usually do this for free or for a nominal fee. Ideally, it should be loose enough to move around your finger but tight enough not to slip over the knuckle without a tug. Bear in mind that your fingers swell in hot weather.

5 Ensure that you get a proper receipt that includes information about the stone's weight and a description of its cut, as well as the price.

INITIAL BIG DAY DECISIONS

Everyone will tell you that you need to start planning early. And they are right. But don't let them press-gang you into hasty judgements. In the months to come the whole affair will feel like a roller-coaster so it pays to take things slowly at the start – particularly since the decisions you make at the earliest stage will create a framework for your wedding day.

ENGAGEMENT PARTIES

- You've already got the mother of all events to organise so these days an engagement party is definitely optional rather than obligatory, particularly if there is a short gap between engagement and wedding.
- Your parents may have different ideas about the way things are done and it is probably easier to give in with good grace if they decide to hold something in your honour, particularly if they are determined to organise and pay for it. If you are footing the bill

for the engagement bash then try to keep the party in perspective. It is not the main event so it isn't essential, for instance, to have champagne on tap or pay for every drink – most guests will want to contribute as they know how expensive weddings are. Go for something informal if you can – a meeting at a pub, bar or restaurant or a low-key 'bring a bottle' party at your home are all good options (also ensuring you don't pick up an enormous bar tab at the end of the evening).

- Many couples opt to have more than one party – that way, your elderly maiden aunt can sip her dry sherry and chat to you about the dress without witnessing the would-be stag night crew practising their wilder drinking moves in the corner.
- One key thing to remember is that everyone who is invited to your engagement party should also come to your wedding. The only honourable exceptions to this rule are work colleagues; it is fine to arrange informal drinks after work so they can celebrate your good news. This can also be done at any time, but a few days before the wedding is most appropriate as this gives them a chance to wish you good luck and calm your pre-wedding jitters.

✦ TALKING DATES

Once you've said 'I do' it's easy to let the months pass by in a haze. But be warned, the questions will start almost immediately and you will get tired of giving endless non-committal answers long before your friends and family tire of asking for dates. You don't have to be press-ganged into any sort of firm arrangement, but it helps to have some vague ideas – starting points if you like.

How long between engagement and marriage?

Long engagements have been the butt of many a sitcom joke, but a generation or two ago it was quite usual to have a three- or four-year gap between getting engaged and walking up the aisle, often so that the couple could save up for their first home. Indeed 'courting' was almost a recognised status. These days engagements don't generally last as long – particularly since so many couples have swapped 'being engaged' for living together. It is absolutely your decision to set the date of your marriage but if you want a popular summer Saturday at a particular venue you may have to book up to a year in advance. And if you want to get married quickly, there are a few legalities you need to bear in mind.

Civil ceremonies

- The absolute minimum between engagement and marriage is determined by law at 15 clear days from the day you meet the registrar. This means if you meet them on 1 July the marriage can take place on 17 July.
- A notice (see page 65) is granted, which gives you the right to marry within a twelve-month period.

Church ceremonies

- For marriages in an Anglican church you need to speak to the vicar. The banns (see page 65) will be called on three consecutive Sundays before the day of your ceremony. There is usually no need to involve the local registrar.
- If you are applying for a special licence to marry in an Anglican church – for instance to marry in a parish where you are not resident but have a long-standing family connection – allow as much time as possible as these have to be approved by the Archbishop of Canterbury. Licences can be granted up to 18 months ahead of the wedding.
- For all other religious faiths you need to speak to the person in charge of marriages at your chosen wedding venue. In most circumstances you will then have to give notice to the registrar and follow the same protocols as for a civil ceremony.

✧ MAKING FIRST PLANS

At this stage you might be suffering from information overload. Everyone is offering advice and asking questions when you may not even have decided how you want to get married. The most useful thing you can do at this stage is make a tentative outline of the sort of day you want. Later on you can fill in the gaps and there's advice on more detailed planning in Chapter 2.

For this first wedding wishlist to work you need to sit down with your partner and a blank piece of paper – a valuable exercise because it will help determine if both of you are thinking along the same lines. One crucial point though: don't involve anyone else at this stage. It is all too easy for an over-excited father of the bride or mother of the groom to start offering ideas. Let them muscle in at this stage and three months down the line it will have been transformed into their wedding and not yours.

What to consider

Checklists – you are going to get used to these in the coming months! – are the best way of starting the planning process off. Now you have your blank piece of paper, here are the questions you need to ponder:

- **Where should we get married?** Your basic preference, from religious building or register office to hotel, theme park, or even the bottom of the ocean.
- **When is the best time?** A chance to consider work commitments, the best time to ensure important guests can be there and also to decide if you prefer to be a summer or winter bride and groom.

WHAT IF WE DON'T AGREE?

Don't panic. Just because one of you wants a pony and trap and the other fancies turning up on a Harley Davidson, it doesn't make you incompatible life partners. The best thing you can do is to discuss your differences and ask questions. Finding out why your partner had a certain vision in their head is a good start – and telling them what you had imagined will help them to understand your point of view. You are both going to have to make compromises on something here, but keep your differences in perspective. It helps if you remember that these are just 'trappings' and not the point of the day.

- **How big/expensive?** The wedding will almost invariably become bigger and more costly than you originally intended, but start on the right footing by estimating guest list numbers and totting up the kind of money you are prepared to spend.
- **What sort of event?** The other three questions you've answered are already setting the tone, but here you should consider the duration of the party, level of formality and also map out a few rough ideas, for instance disco v. classical string quartet, canapés v. hog roast.

TROUBLESHOOTING

✧ SECOND AND MATURE MARRIAGES

'I'm hardly the blushing young bride and my husband-to-be is a widower. We want to have a proper wedding celebration without it feeling too traditional or stuffy.'

Every wedding is different and you actually have more freedom to design the one you want than many other couples – especially since you are not tied to the trappings of a white dress and huge family reception. There are elements to consider that will make the day feel less formal but still ensure you feel properly married.

1 First decide on the sort of service you want. Not all religious services take place in a hail of confetti on a Saturday; you could explore other options, such as a weekday or afternoon-into-evening event. You have to be married before 6pm, but this can be atmospheric and sophisticated, particularly if you adjourn to a restaurant afterwards or host a cocktail party at home.
2 For civil ceremonies a hotel, golf club or other 'wedding package' venue may be the best option if you want a less traditional twist to the proceedings. This also offers you scope for introducing your own individuality to proceedings. With all civil ceremonies, alongside the formal wordings you can include your own vows,

introduce readings or poetry and frame the event with favourite secular music.

3 Although you still need witnesses to the marriage itself, you can avoid all the usual speeches and wedding lines at the reception if you prefer to keep things low-key. You may still want to include toasts – perhaps one from the bride and groom and one from each of your witnesses or someone close to you such as children, siblings or close mutual friends.

4 The typical dress code at weddings is a 20th-century invention' and there is no need to wear white or insist on starched collars for the men. In fact, your best choice is the one that makes you feel most comfortable. For instance, at an evening event you could go for glamorous evening dress and ask male guests to wear dinner jackets to make the party feel sophisticated rather than stuffy. For daytime services – even in church – shorter dresses are perfectly appropriate and men can wear suits or smart trousers and jackets. Avoid hats, head-dresses and bouquets and your wedding will instantly feel less formal.

✧ INCLUDING OUR CHILDREN

'We're both getting married for the second time and we want to include our children from previous relationships in the event. How do we manage this without making them (or us) feel uncomfortable?'

It is important to let your children get involved in the celebration, as it is a big event for them too. But you need to tread carefully and also respect their views. A lot depends on their age and their attitude to the impending remarriage. After all, they are gaining a whole new family – including siblings.

1 Start by talking to them and letting them feel involved in the planning. Younger children may go along with proceedings quite happily – especially if they have a special role such as bridesmaids or pages. Be scrupulously fair so that both sets of children feel they are equally valued and involved in the event.

2 If your children are teenagers, you may face the twin obstacles of
self-consciousness and resistance to anyone moving in to
Dad/Mum's territory. Don't court trouble by telling them how to
behave. Instead, explain how much you want them to be part of
your day. See if you can find a special role that doesn't involve
them in too much embarrassment. For instance, they could act as
ushers or help out with greeting the guests.

3 If your children are older still (18+) then perhaps you could ask
them to be your witnesses. This is an important symbolic role and
demonstrates to them how much you value their moral support. It
also shows that you recognise them as adults.

4 Do make sure that your children sit on the top table if this is to
be a formal event. Also remember to mention them publicly. Both
you and your spouse should make a special mention in your
speeches. Thank your own children for their support and your
partner's for welcoming you into this 'new and extended' family.
This thoughtfulness may not guarantee an easy ride post wedding
day but it will go a long way to ensuring that they all know how
much you consider their feelings.

✧ CHOOSING SOMEONE TO GIVE ME AWAY

'My father died recently and I'm not sure how to arrange things at
the wedding. Can I choose someone else to give me away?'

**Going up the aisle on your father's arm is something you are
going to miss sorely on your wedding day. But there are other
people who can step into the role, you just need to decide on the
best choice for you.**

1 Technically, any close family member can give you away – it's
down to you to decide on the best person. You need to consider
who would fulfil the role best and make you feel most
comfortable.

2 Typical choices to fulfil this role are a mother, uncle, godfather or
brother. Ask them well in advance as they are taking on a big role

in your wedding if they agree. You may also ask them to give a
speech at the reception, although this is not essential.

3 It might be a good idea to discuss this with your mother and find
out her opinion. Remember that she might find the sight of you
going up the aisle on someone else's arm particularly hard to bear.
She may also have her own preference and perhaps this is one
occasion where you should allow her to have first say.

4 If you feel uncomfortable about handing over the role that is
traditionally held by the bride's father it might be better to split
the duties. For instance, an uncle could lead you up the aisle
and your mother, brother and godfather could all make short
speeches. Of course, those speeches should include some
reference to the absence of your father on this special day.

✧ DECIDING WHO TAKES CENTRE STAGE

'My father, who left home when I was three, has offered to pay for
my wedding – on condition he gives me away. I'm not sure how to
react, or what to tell my mother and stepfather.'

**Your father is using cash to persuade you to let him take centre
stage. Put that offer to one side while you consider where your
true loyalties lie.**

1 If you are still very close to your father and would prefer him to
give you away, then you are fine accepting his offer but need to
be ultra-diplomatic in explaining this to your mother and
stepfather. Ensure you give them key supporting roles – as
speech-makers, witnesses or chief reception line hosts.

2 If you are not close to your father, then decide how important his
cash really is and also consider what other 'strings' are attached.
Does it mean he expects to become much closer to you in the
future or that you will end up feeling beholden?

3 Now think about the impact on your mother. She could have an
uncomfortable day if he takes on a 'starring' role. Also consider
your stepfather. If he brought you up and would have been your

first choice to give you away then you risk damaging your future relationship.

4 If you do decide to turn down your father's offer you may find he still wants to help out financially, and he should be invited as a top-table guest. However, if he refuses to come and withdraws his offer of financial assistance, then you will know you have made the right decision.

CHAPTER 2

FIRST WEDDING PLANS

Choices, choices, added to the weight of other people's expectations, can make planning your wedding a daunting task. So the best way to minimise the stress is to narrow down your options as soon as you can. It's important to think positively, so view this not as an overwhelming decision-making process but as a golden opportunity to be creative and organise an event that is uniquely yours. Here you'll find the first essentials of event management: timings, guest lists and budgets.

FIXING A DATE

Committing a date to paper is the initial decision you need to make. Just about everything else you organise depends on this, so think of it as the first piece in the jigsaw puzzle. You could just pick a lucky number out of a hat, but it makes sense to answer four basic questions first.

- **Can I secure my venue/s?** This is your starting point if you're looking to marry in late spring or summer in a popular and picturesque location. Remember that some venues get booked up more than a year in advance. The safest option is to shortlist several dates and possibly have more than one venue in the frame. If you're more flexible about the wedding venue then move on to question two.

- **Is it a good time for work/essential commitments?** If you know you have a mad season coming up at work then it makes sense to avoid planning a wedding in the middle of it. Even if you make it up the aisle successfully you will look every inch the frazzled executive rather than a beautiful bride/handsome groom. Be realistic and choose a time when both of you will feel relaxed enough to enjoy the party.

- **Can the major players make it?** Not everybody you invite will be able to attend, but you are going to want the support of close family/friends. Tentative questions need to be asked of parents, siblings and bosom buddies. The best way to do this is to come up with three or four potential dates and then synchronise diaries. If you have friends on the other side of the world that you want to invite then you need to talk to them early – especially since most of the long-haul flight deals need to be booked months in advance.

- **Will there be time to organise everything?** If you're planning a quick wedding then do be realistic about dates. Remember the time taken to fulfil legalities (see Talking dates, Chapter 1 page 18). Also consider practicalities for the rest of your guests; they need to make arrangements for your wedding too and this could be difficult if you give them less than three months' notice.

YOUR FIRST SIX-POINT 'TO DO' LIST

You need a calm and ordered approach rather than a mad panic to survive the first major planning stage. The good news is there's a logical and time-honoured priority order for making the major decisions – stick to it and you won't suddenly find you've set a wedding date with no prospect of a decent reception venue nearby. Fine tune details only after you've put this framework into place. The six essentials are listed here in priority order; you'll find more information about the points you need to consider before finalising each stage in the rest of this chapter. (For a more detailed wedding planner, see Chapter 4 page 84.)

☐ Fix wedding date
☐ Confirm budget
☐ Agree style of wedding
☐ Book wedding venue/organise legalities
☐ Book reception venue/catering
☐ Draw up guest list

A NOTE ABOUT TIMINGS: The longer you have to arrange your wedding the better, but it's perfectly possible to organise everything in under three months if you are prepared to be flexible about wedding and reception times. The key essentials are the marriage and reception venues – get those confirmed and you can relax and start shopping for your wedding finery.

✧ WHICH SEASON?

- **Spring** The weather can be gorgeous when the blossom is out, but there are also grey days and spring showers to contend with. If you plan a church service, you need to avoid the period around Lent.
- **Summer** Marquees and strawberries (or summer downpours if you get unlucky). But from mid-July onwards, you are into peak holiday season so you may find some of your guests are on vacation. Also remember that almost three quarters of weddings are booked for late spring–summer, which means venue and caterer availability goes down and prices shoot up.
- **Autumn** A sunny day in late September or October can be picture perfect, but the weather is more variable. That said, you have fewer problems with holidays and more availability of wedding venues. Prices also tend to go down.

- **Winter** Romantic if you have candlelight and winter foliage dressing your venue and you have the chance to dress in sumptuous velvet or cashmere. But the days are short (a key issue if you have a photographer in tow) and for church marriages you need to shoehorn your service in around Advent/Christmas worship.

True life stories: Own goal

Julie thought she had covered most bases when she fixed the date for her wedding to Owen. However, in the flurry of preparations a year ahead of time she'd forgotten to consult a sporting fixture list, although – to be fair – neither of them had predicted that Wales would still be in with a chance of winning rugby's Six Nations title. Owen's family and friends tried to keep their minds on the service but during the reception people kept slipping off to watch the TV and several guests had smuggled in carefully concealed radios. 'It turned into the party of all parties in the end, but before the full-time whistle you could almost cut the air with a knife,' says Julie. 'I think it would have turned into a wake if Wales hadn't won, but at least everyone remembers our wedding fondly. A couple of guests told me it was the happiest day of their life!'

DID YOU KNOW...? OPEN 365 DAYS A YEAR

While Saturday is the favourite day of the week for weddings, you can marry in church on any day of the year (including the big religious holidays) if the vicar or priest agrees to it. By law you must be married between the hours of 8am and 6pm in a church or approved wedding venue, while register offices only let you tie the knot up to 4pm during the week and 1pm at weekends. In Scotland, the rules are more liberal, although the priest or official presiding will have to agree to your proposed time. Jewish and Quaker weddings are the only exception to the general rule, as these are allowed to take place in the evenings.

BUDGETS – WHO PAYS?

With the average British wedding costing over £12,000, it's little wonder that splitting the bill has become more popular. But before you assess your finances, here are some tips on managing the tricky topic of money.

- **Start by fixing a budget** If you start the other way round (hiring venue, choosing dress and so on) you'll get a nasty shock midway through the organisation. It's vital to do some clear thinking about cash right from the start. You need to decide how much you and your partner will each be contributing and where this money is coming from. Do be realistic about costs and include a contingency fund (10–15 per cent) for overspends. If you need to arrange finance, this should be tackled as early as possible so you can shop around for the best-value loan. (See Raising funds, page 31.)

- **Find out who else is contributing** Parents and relatives often want to become involved and – once they have mentioned helping out with the finances – you need to discuss their contributions with them, ideally face to face. You and your partner need to display tact, so this is one occasion when you should avoid putting both sets of parents in the same room together. If one side can/is willing to contribute more than the other this can cause embarrassment or even ill-feeling. You also want to avoid one set of parents feeling press-ganged into offering more than they can reasonably afford. If there is a big disparity between contributions, keep this quiet and accept both sides' money gratefully.

- **Gather costings on their behalf** Sometimes parents or relatives talk not in terms of contributing money, but funding one aspect of the wedding. This is not a blank cheque, so if someone has expressed a wish to 'sort out the flowers' then it is up to you to go back to them with a reasonably accurate costing and make a compromise if necessary. They might have thought of a light sprinkling of in-season daffodils not huge bunches of orchids flown in from the hothouses of Kenya – an important distinction that needs to be clarified early.

- **Set up an accounting system** Sounds boring, but it is vital that all monies you pay over in deposits, down payments and the like are recorded in an accounting book (an A5 lined pad will do if you can't face a formal spreadsheet). Not only does this ensure you keep track of who has been paid what, it also guarantees that no resentment builds up between you and your partner. It is all too easy, in the tension of planning, for one side to feel all the financial burden is falling on them. The accounts book can be reviewed regularly to keep things straight between you.

DID YOU KNOW...? WHO USED TO FOOT THE BILL

Financing a wedding used to be a straightforward business – for the groom's side. While they handled the church/marriage fees and the honeymoon (more likely to be a week at the British seaside than a South Sea island), the bride's father had to dig deep to finance all the reception costs. And the bride's side was out of pocket in other ways too, since women normally embarked on married life armed with a packed 'trousseau' containing enough household linen and 'smalls' to last until the silver wedding anniversary.

✧ RAISING FUNDS

Organising a wedding is a costly business if you are paying for it yourselves, so many couples take out a loan. The temptation is to take an easy option – and many lenders are all too willing to fuel your shopping spree – but it is worth spending time tracking down the best finance deal. If you own your home, the cheapest source of lending could be your mortgage provider as you are negotiating an additional loan secured against your property. A standard bank loan, which isn't secured, is more expensive but may still be cheaper than racking up debt on your credit card. If you do go for the credit card option, shop around for an interest free offer and apply for a new card to pay for all expenses (useful as you'll also be able to keep track of accounts). Just remember that you will have a deadline to pay the money back and then the costs will soar.

TEN WAYS TO ECONOMISE

No one can criticise you for wanting to plan the best party ever, but if your initial calculations show you will be paying off the wedding until retirement day it's time to cut your cloth accordingly. Here are ten ways to shave that budget.

1 **Cut the guest list** Yes, it hurts, but it is the most obvious way to shave hundreds off your budget. If you can't cut it, consider a split reception and give the evening guests a finger buffet/canapés rather than the works.

2 **Give them less to eat** You want to host a feast, but are four courses really necessary, particularly on a hot summer's day? Consider offering two courses instead or switching to the buffet option (always cheaper due to fewer serving staff). If you want an even sneakier way of ensuring you don't have to feed and water your guests for many hours start the celebration later. A 4pm wedding rather than a lunchtime affair ensures you only have to provide one round of food and give them less to drink.

3 **Shave your bar bill** Vintage champagne will be wasted on most of your guests after the first glass, so switch to sparkling or still wine. Or water things down by serving Buck's Fizz. Remember to have soft drinks on display; many guests will be thirsty, but not necessarily for alcohol. If you think the tab is still going to cripple you, introduce a pay bar after the first couple of drinks – no one will mind. If you're catering at home, consider a booze cruise to France to stock up on drinks at bargain prices.

4 **Hire your wedding outfits** Many grooms rent their morning suit or tuxedo, but this is also an increasingly popular option for brides. You don't have a dress to wrap in tissue paper for your heirs, but do they want your old dress anyway? The real plus point of hiring is that you can get to wear the ultimate designer frock at a fraction of the cost of buying it forever.

5 **Limit bridesmaids/pages** If you don't have oodles of delightful nieces and nephews then bridesmaids can look a bit out of place anyway. You can get married without them or just have one star attendant in your wake. Also remember that the bridesmaid (or her mother) might be happy to pay for her own dress.

6 **Borrow transport** If you know someone with a smart saloon, a choice classic/vintage car or even a pony and trap, consider enlisting their help to get you to the church, chapel or register office. It's an easy economy, you can dress up the transport with bunting or balloons, and not many guests will be focusing on your motor anyway (hopefully).

7 **Cut back on photos** There are endless creative ways to do this and not having 30 minutes of awkwardly posed group shots can be a blessed relief. Consider getting the photographer to take just essential shots of bride and groom with respective family/friends. Then issue disposable cameras to your guests and ask them to hand over the cameras at the end of the day. Or enlist the help of a photographer guest with a decent digital camera. Ensure he or she carries a spare memory card.

8 **Limit the flowers** Florist's bills can be a major expense if you get too carried away with church decorations, reception centrepieces and bouquets/buttonholes. See if you can use the same flowers for church and reception or share flowers with the wedding before or after you. Choose in-season blooms (your florist can advise) and introduce cheaper greenery.

9 **Let a friend DJ** Everyone knows someone who loves to take over the party music and this is his or her chance for a starring role. All you need is two hired speakers and a decent MP3 player to get the party onto the dance floor. One word of warning though: choose a friend with catholic taste and a large music collection rather than someone who only owns garage/raga/ thrash metal.

10 **Host a DIY reception** Sometimes the simplest celebrations are the best ones and it's perfectly possible to buy or hire a marquee for your back garden and find excellent celebration food in the major supermarkets or local delicatessen. Yes it's the budget option, but most of your guests will love it just as much and you will save a fortune. You may even find that guests are willing to chip in with homemade trifles, cakes and other signature dishes.

True life stories: We did it our way

When Candy and Michael decided to get married on the spur of the moment they barely had time to organise the register office, let alone plan a proper reception. Their solution was nothing if not seat-of-the-pants creative.
'I managed to borrow an off-the-peg dress from a local designer with the promise I would tell all my friends about her on the day,' says Candy.
A friend drove them to the register office in his vintage sports car and guests were all asked to bring a bottle plus one salad or desert capable of feeding up to 15 people. 'It worked because it was summer salad season,' says Michael.
'We set up the barbecue in the back garden, everyone took turns to mind the sausages and we all ate like lords. Everyone loved the informality.'

DECIDING WHERE TO MARRY

This creates the framework for your day so it's the most important decision you need to make. While it used to be a straight church v. civil option, now you can opt for the whole package by selecting a hotel, historic house or other approved wedding venue.

Church/religious building

Pros: Nothing matches the atmosphere of a place of worship and it is the obvious choice if you have a strong religious commitment or family tie to a particular place. You will also find that more traditionally minded guests feel that you are 'truly married'.

Cons: You may want/need to fulfil certain commitments by demonstrating that you worship at the church, have a religious faith or a strong tie to the place you want to be married. The diaries of places of worship may also get filled well ahead of time, particularly during 'marrying season'. You may find the service is inflexible and old fashioned.

Register office

Pros: It's easy to arrange a civil wedding in a register office, and also quick if you are planning a whirlwind occasion. You have scope to add in personal touches such as your own music and poetry readings. The atmosphere is less solemn than a church.

Cons: Some – though not all – register offices can feel soulless and there may be the feeling of a production line, particularly if you marry at a busy time. Services are short, so you may find you and your guests are back on the street before the hankies have come out. You are not allowed to introduce religious messages or music into the proceedings however close they are to your heart.

Approved wedding venue

Pros: Offers you the 'one stop shop' so that guests can move seamlessly from the marriage to the reception. Since you choose the place (which must have a licence as an 'approved wedding venue'), you can tailor the whole event round a particular mood or theme. Less hassle is involved in transporting guests or organising timings.

Cons: Since you have to buy the whole package this can be an expensive option. You are in the wedding venue's hands so are reliant on them to ensure the organisation is up to scratch. Popular wedding venues will be booked up well ahead of time. Civil marriage rules apply so the service must be secular.

DID YOU KNOW...? YOUR RIGHT TO A CHURCH WEDDING

Technically, everyone in the UK has the right to marry in their parish church, whether or not they were baptised or attend services. The only exclusions are divorcees or under-age couples. If you would like a church wedding local to your home but aren't sure of your eligibility, your first move should be to contact your local priest.

✧ ADDING PERSONAL TOUCHES TO YOUR WEDDING

Introducing personal vows is a wonderful way to make your wedding feel truly special. Although many other faiths are more liberal in their approach to wedding vows, at an Anglican or Catholic ceremony you are required to stick to a fairly strict wording (although brides may decide whether or not to 'obey' their partner). To get round this, most couples introduce personal touches through hymns, readings and the processional music they choose for entering and leaving the church. The amount of freedom you are given depends on the minister but non-religious readings and music – from Winnie the Pooh to the theme from *Titanic* – are often allowed provided they don't upset the vicar. At civil ceremonies you have far more freedom; once you have said the legally binding part of the ceremony you can add vows, poems or statements that express your own personal feelings about each other. The only thing to remember is that all aspects of the service must be non-religious and your registrar also needs to approve your choices in advance. For total freedom, opt for a humanist service. This is not legally binding but can be combined with a register office wedding. A humanist celebrant will help you write your own service, which can take place anywhere you choose, including outdoors. Fees are normally around £300 plus travel. Contact the British Humanist Association for more information.

✧ FORMAL OR INFORMAL?

Most couples pick and choose the elements they consider most important, so don't feel it's a straight decision between champagne reception and the saloon bar of your local. But there are four key elements that you can play with to make the event feel more or less formal:

- **Venue/s** A religious ceremony feels more formal than a civil ceremony because of the strict protocols and the fact that even avowed atheists tend to be awed by the atmosphere in a church or other religious building. But there are no hard and fast rules on this one and it rather depends on the venue you choose afterwards for the reception. For instance, formality becomes timeless country-style simplicity if you combine a simple country church with a marquee in the garden. And if you want chic sophistication combine a service in a city register office with a reception in a boutique hotel or smart restaurant.
- **Size of guest list** The more people you invite the more time they will spend introducing themselves to each other and that is bound to add to the awkwardness of the event. People also tend to behave in a more grown-up fashion in front of strangers. This could be a very good thing if you want to curb your family/friends' wild side and ensure the day doesn't end in a fight/stripping contest. But if you are looking for excuses to limit the guest list or split proceedings into day/evening receptions then this is a cast-iron one. (For more details see Drawing up a guest list, page 38.)
- **Dress code** A wedding is an opportunity for everyone to shop for new clothes. However, introduce the words 'morning dress' on the invitation and your male contingent will be strait-jacketed into hot

and generally hired outfits for the day, while the women will spend hours trying to find a hat that doesn't make them look like their mother. That said, formal dress creates a marvellous sense of occasion and looks incredibly photogenic, so it's your call. One less formal alternative is to ensure the key players (groom, immediate family, best man, ushers) wear morning dress and allow guests the option of 'lounge suit' (a standard suit in any colour other than black). This also reduces guest expenditure considerably.

- **Reception** A greeting line and seated reception can feel stuffy, particularly if you have a four-course meal and a long round of speeches before the guests can leave their seats. But you can do a

FANCY SOMETHING DIFFERENT?

Since the civil wedding rules were relaxed in the early 1990s, a whole host of unlikely places have stepped forward to offer their services as wedding venues. You will still need a registrar to preside over the ceremony, but here are some ideas for tying the knot in your own unique style.

Good morning campers You can say i (de hi) do at a holiday camp, which offers the benefit of overnight accommodation for your guests and entertainment for the children. Some even lay on special features such as an Elvis impersonator to serenade you down the aisle.

See the sights Many of London's top tourist destinations offer wedding packages, including the Natural History Museum, Tower Bridge and the London Eye. You can even get hitched on a river cruise along the Thames. A great day out for your guests, although you may not be the centre of attention!

Join the animals Zoos and wildlife parks offer guaranteed entertainment for adults and children and a unique soundtrack for your special day (roaring lions, bellowing baboons, etc.). Chester Zoo and Whipsnade are among the popular choices.

Sporting legends If the chance to marry on the sacred home turf is too good an opportunity to miss, check out the packages at your football club. Many offer ceremonies on the pitch itself, which means no trouble inviting a large crowd of supporters. Rugby and cricket clubs and racecourses are alternative options if one of those is your preferred sport.

(For a comprehensive list of unusual and mainstream wedding venues, check out the Confetti website, see Useful Sources, page 120.)

lot to create a more relaxed atmosphere. For instance, it is perfectly acceptable to limit the reception line to bride and groom only, or forgo it altogether. You can opt for a buffet to give guests a chance to mingle or, if you choose a sit-down meal, consider alternative seating plans such as opting for round rather than rectangular tables. Another useful icebreaker is to allow guests to sit where they like or allot them a table but not a fixed place. (For more details on planning your reception see Seating plan, Chapter 5 page 98.)

DRAWING UP A GUEST LIST

Guests make your party, so little wonder this is every wedding organiser's waking nightmare. Not only do you have to start by deciding who to include (and who to leave out), but you may then find yourself editing furiously and striking people off 'the list' because that intimate gathering has turned into a monster bash.

✧ PLAYING THE NAME GAME

There is no easy place to start with a guest list, but it is a good idea to start writing down names early – at least a month before you plan to send out your invitations. This allows you time to fine-tune numbers, dig out people's last-known address and argue the point over his/her friends you can't stand.

Most guest lists are restricted by space and/or the size of the budget so it is important to be realistic from the start. Remember that any wedding venue will have a strict maximum dictated by fire regulations and it's essential to get this confirmed before you start issuing invitations. And even if you are holding a knees-up in a private home you will want to manage numbers, for practicality and safety's sake.

Don't expect to get the list in perfect order at the first attempt – there will be people you forget. Also check that you've included absolutely everyone in the final figure – including the bride and groom! Once you've agreed the list together, it's worth handing it over to parents/siblings just in case you've neglected to invite dear old Uncle Albert or forgotten that Auntie Sadie is no longer married to the person you're about to include in her invitation. (For details of how to word your invitation, and what other information to include, see Wedding invitations, Chapter 4 page 67.)

A- and B-lists

There will be refusals, so most couples have an A- and B-list in operation. Usually this is no reflection on the value of the friendship – more that you are obliged to invite certain people, even if it is unlikely they will make it. The best way to keep things running smoothly is to make sure you send out all the 'must dos' (aged aunt who never leaves home, best friend in Outer Mongolia) as early as you possibly can. Once you have received his or her refusal, you have cleared a space for someone you know is more likely to come. For obvious reasons, it is essential no one ever finds out they were on your B-list, so be careful not to give the game away by sending out an A-list invitation to someone who is close friends with a B-lister. It's better to hold both invitations back, rather than send one ages after the other.

Giving parents their say

If parents are big contributors to the cost of the wedding then they can reasonably expect to have input into both the size and scope of the guest list. This can be a source of tension, particularly if there are people you barely know invited because your parents went to their son/daughter's wedding. This is one of those times when you realise a wedding day is not just about you and the sensible course is to give in with good grace. If parents aren't stumping up cash, it is still a generous and grown-up move to listen to their viewpoint and concede to at least some of their wishes. Look at it this way: they will get much more pride and pleasure out of the day if they feel their close friends/relatives are sharing it with them. You will, however, need to display a fair degree of tact if their requests are getting wildly out of hand.

Point out gently that numbers are limited and there are people you feel must take priority because they are close to you or your partner. Offer to put their extra requests onto your B-list if that helps smooth things over.

Big family meets little family

Guest lists have a nasty habit of spiralling out of control when one partner comes from a modest/manageable family but the other has a vast tribe of relatives. The problems this can cause are twofold. First, you have a huge bill to pay unless you keep numbers in check. Second, you risk one side being so completely dwarfed by the other that the whole wedding feels 'unbalanced'. You will also have issues to cope with such as seating plans at the reception and church. If things can't be resolved easily here are some possible solutions.

- **Make some rules** The best way around the problem is to talk about it and decide on some rules, such as, 'No second cousins from either side allowed'.
- **Have a split reception** Having a small wedding breakfast for close friends and family and then allowing in more people for an evening reception is a useful way to bypass the numbers issue, particularly if you have hordes of cousins or teenage nieces and nephews. The dim lights and loud music of an evening party means people won't notice the imbalance in the guest list. You may also find that some older relatives make their excuses and leave once the crowds hit the dance floor.
- **Have an informal reception** A buffet or finger food reception will mask the fact that one side has far fewer relatives than the other, particularly if you add in plenty of mutual friends. It's also a good way to keep costs down.
- **Invite adults only** Sometimes an adults-only rule is the only way to ensure you get all the people you want at the wedding. Some guests may grumble, but provided the ruling is fair to both sides, you should be able to justify your decision.

True life stories: Musical chairs

When Nick and Jenny started planning their reception they were faced by the prospect of putting two large families together who had never really met each other. 'We just knew that it could make the day feel very formal and strained and we wanted to make things more relaxed,' says Jenny. Their solution was to introduce a formal seating plan but then ask male guests to swap tables after each course. 'It caused headaches for the caterers, but we explained why we were doing it and they were very accommodating,' adds Jenny. 'Some guests were a bit stuffy about moving, but by dessert everyone was getting along famously.'

TROUBLESHOOTING

✦ MARRYING IN OUR DREAM CHURCH

'I've always dreamed of getting married in a lovely village church and I've found the perfect place – but neither of us lives in the parish. What do I have to do to persuade the vicar to marry us?'

If you are both free to marry and Anglican (presuming this is a CofE church) then technically you can apply to marry in the parish of your choosing. But it isn't as straightforward as that, so be prepared to fulfil some important criteria.

1 Start attending church there. It's not a couple of brief appearances though – you might typically be expected to attend over a period of six months before your wedding. It's a good idea to be visible too, so make yourselves known to the parish priest and other parishioners.

2 It's important to let the priest know your wishes at an early stage – and be prepared to answer tough questions about why you want to marry in this church rather than in your own parish. Think through your reasons carefully. Does it have some family or childhood connection? Is it a special place because of its peaceful/joyous atmosphere? This sort of reasoning will have far

more sway than telling the minister 'because it will look wonderful in the photos'!

3 Provided the minister agrees in principle, he or she will then want to discuss your plans with you and may ask you to attend marriage preparation discussions covering topics such as family, children and communicating with each other.

4 Once you've attended the church for a satisfactory period of time you can be entered onto the parish's electoral roll, which qualifies you to marry there. You will still have to go through the process of banns – so allow a month or more for this legality.

5 In certain circumstances you can forgo the church attendance rules and marry in a church outside your own parish. Be warned though, at present you need to apply for a special licence from the Archbishop of Canterbury and these are usually only granted if someone has a genuine (e.g. family) connection to a church. There is an ongoing discussion about relaxing this ruling within the next three years, but that is a long time to wait, even if it does happen.

✧ SAYING 'I DO' ON A TROPICAL BEACH

'We just don't think we can bear the whole process of planning a big family wedding – a tropical beach sounds far more inviting.'

Swapping veil for flip-flops is an increasingly popular option – you get the marriage and honeymoon in one and the ultimate in sun-drenched wedding snaps. But you do need to plan this style of wedding just as carefully. Here are some pointers.

1 The ceremony isn't going to happen if you don't take the right paperwork with you. Different countries have very different rules and you will almost certainly need to supply birth certificates, plus if one of you has been married before they will need proof that the marriage is legally ended (decree absolute or partner's death certificate). You will also need to ensure you have more than six months to run on your current passport. Check all legal requirements thoroughly with the embassy of the country where

you intend to marry. You may also be required – or decide it's a good idea – to visit the embassy in person, to ensure all the paperwork is in place.

2 Many couples opt for a specialist travel agency after realising the paperwork involved (see above) and this is a sensible idea if you don't fancy the idea of long-distance planning. Check the credentials of your travel agency carefully and take out travel/wedding insurance as extra security.

3 While the 'fly, marry' option may sound good on paper, you need time to get over your flight, acclimatise to the food and heat and possibly satisfy residency requirements in the country where you are having your wedding. Again, check with the country's embassy or your travel agency.

4 Work out what you need to take with you in the way of outfits, etc. and see if the airline will allow you to carry the essentials as hand luggage. It would be a terrible shame if your dress ended up languishing in Montevideo, while you were in Rio.

5 What about witnesses? It may sound romantic to gather two wizened fishermen from the beach, but do you really want strangers sharing your special moment rather than your sister/best friend/parents?

6 If the answer to question five is 'No' and you want guests, then you need to consider how they will make it to the wedding. Are you prepared to help fund flights/accommodation, or at least shop around for travel deals? Also remember that some elderly relatives may find the idea of jetting halfway round the world a terrifying ordeal, so it may not be fair to even ask them to come.

7 If you do have guests then they may be gatecrashing your honeymoon. Some couples slip off after the wedding to another location – worth considering if you want quality time together.

8 Still convinced? Then this sounds like a great idea for your wedding. If you can't invite many guests – or they can't afford to come – do consider hosting an informal party for them on your return. They won't want to feel cheated out of celebrating your marriage and you will want to show off your tan!

✧ MIXING WEDDING TRADITIONS

'My partner is Catholic and I'm Hindu, how do we accommodate our different traditions and satisfy our respective families?'

You want to share your lives together, that's the important thing. Most cultural/religious differences can be accommodated in a legal wedding service. You just need to find a formula that works for you as a couple.

1 If you want any sort of religious service – of either faith – you need to talk to the priests at your local temple/church. But before you get that far it's a good idea to sit down together and decide on the 'rules of engagement'. Are you prepared for two religious services or do you favour one over the other? Each priest will tell you what he is prepared/allowed to do and most will do their best to help accommodate you. You might expect a few tricky questions though, most notably what faith any children you may have will adopt. Remember that you will still have to inform the registrar and go through civil preliminaries.

2 A civil wedding in a register office or wedding venue is a simple option if you want to be legally married without feeling either side's traditions are being ignored. Since this is a civil ceremony there is no religious content, although you should find the registrar sympathetic to the introduction of readings or music that introduce both cultural traditions into the day.

3 If you want to set the seal on your day you could also host a humanist service. This allows you scope to be far more personal and express your own beliefs within a non-denominational setting. This needs to be combined with a civil ceremony but can take place on a different day if you prefer (see Adding personal touches to your wedding, page 35).

4 Whatever option sounds best, do talk to your respective parents about the decision-making process and perhaps enlist their help if you want a religious service (they may have more sway with the local priest). The important thing to remember is that both

sides must feel involved, so make sure you celebrate respective cultural traditions.

5 Remember to advise your guests on the style of service; they may find some of the protocols confusing without a steer from you. The most useful way to do this is to draw up some form of order of service to be handed out on arrival. Alternatively, include a note with the invitation so people know what to expect.

6 Be careful when it comes to planning the catering. Choose a menu that will appeal to both Hindu and Catholic guests, bearing in mind dietary/religious requirements and attitudes to spicy or 'unfamiliar' foods. Your caterers should be able to advise you on the fail-safe options.

7 Remember that most people will relish the chance to see different customs and cultures up close. Just make sure you balance your seating arrangements so guests from both families are encouraged to mingle and share the experience.

CHAPTER 3

CHOOSING YOUR SUPPORT TEAM

Appointing your crew of supporters is one of the key decisions you have to make before you get married. In some cases, the best man or bridesmaids are obvious choices, but you will also need a cast of helpers to get you through the stag/hen night and up the aisle on time. Plus, your parents will want to get involved in the excitement.

This chapter helps you ensure you pick the right people and gives useful advice on delegating, organising pre-wedding parties and getting yourself out of trouble if someone gets offended because you didn't (or did) ask them to help.

SELECTING THE 'A' TEAM

This is an occasion where you have to take on the role of team manager; don't pick someone just because you like him or her (although that is essential) but because you know he or she will be up to the job. While you may start off thinking the best man just has to turn up and make a witty speech and the chief bridesmaid is there to stop the bride tripping over her train, there is far more to both jobs than that. And if you choose wisely you will get much-needed support throughout your wedding preparations plus a pair of broad shoulders to help avert crises on the day.

✧ BEST MAN

There may be one person whose name comes to mind straight away. If not, consider splitting the role between two people.

Duties
- Masterminding stag night
- Getting you to the church on time
- Guarding your wedding ring with his life
- Giving the wittiest/most salacious speech
- Organising anything that needs doing on the day

1 The sort of person you need is, primarily, someone you can trust. So that rules out your dearest but most unreliable friend from the start. Your best man needs to be there on the day and have the wit to step into the breach if there aren't enough chairs at the reception, the wine waiter has disappeared or one of your uncles appears to be performing a striptease on the dance floor. A good best man will also show sensitivity by helping elderly ladies to their seats, persuading the most awkward bridesmaid out onto the floor for a first dance and never, ever even thinking of saying something in his speech that will horrify your bride/family. (See Unaccustomed as I am…, Chapter 5 page 102.)
2 Even the most trusted best man may need guidance from you, so it's important to give him a steer on key points – for instance if

you don't want a rowdy rugby-club-style stag night then tell him. If you want his speech to avoid references to your legendary lads' weekend in Amsterdam, former girlfriend or future mother-in-law, then make that plain too. Do check that the person you choose is prepared to stand up there on the day and wow the crowds with his prose. But even more importantly, pick someone with sound judgement and maturity – being stranded in Shetland on your wedding morning with no clothes or money is one of those hilarious ideas that should never come off the drawing board.

True life stories: How one best man survived the speech
When Ed was asked to be Gareth's best man, he relished the party-organising part of his duties, but knew he was going to struggle with the speech. Unused to public speaking, he spent ages working out a way of not only surviving the ordeal, but also doing what a best man is supposed to do and making the crowd laugh. In the end, the solution presented itself. 'We'd played a horrible joke on Gareth at the stag weekend by replacing his suitcase of clothes with another one full of stuff that a man twenty years older and four sizes smaller than him would wear. This meant we had loads of good photos,' says Ed. 'All I had to do was get some commemorative mugs, T-shirts and plates printed and hand them round during my speech. It was great to have props to keep me going and although I flunked my lines a bit the guests were so busy laughing at Gareth I think I got away with it.'

DID YOU KNOW…? THE BEST MAN'S ROLE

While his uses are many and varied, the original role of the best man was as protector of the groom. His chief duty was to ensure he got the groom to church without being waylaid or side-tracked. Even today it is supposed to be bad luck for a bridegroom to turn back if he's forgotten something – although most brides would consider it a risk worth taking if the wedding ring or airline tickets have been left on the kitchen table.

✧ CHIEF BRIDESMAID

Not everyone has a chief bridesmaid (or matron of honour if she's married), but it is a great way of singling out a close friend/sister and also enlisting much-needed back up on the day.

Duties
- Masterminding the hen night
- Following the bride up the aisle
- Managing train/veil/outfit changes etc.
- Holding onto bouquet/tissues/make up/money
- Keeping other attendants (if any) in check

1 The sort of person you need is capable and prepared to star in a supporting role (no upstagers please!). They have to submit to your choice of dress, although it's only fair to let them have a say, particularly if they are paying for it. Chief bridesmaids often organise the hen night or bridal shower and also help on the day by meeting and greeting guests, keeping an eye on unruly small children and – ultimate sacrifice – asking elderly uncles to join them on the dance floor for the Funky Gibbon.

2 A good bridesmaid is also, literally, your maid – they may even have to accompany you to the bathroom if you chose that dress with 27 concealed buttons down the back. So choose someone you trust to notice if your make up has run, your veil is wonky or your straps have slipped. Make sure they won't mind shadowing you for at least part of the day and pick someone who gets on well with the best man – these two should really work as a team. And if you like, you can ask the bridesmaid to give a speech, although this is not part of standard wedding tradition.

✧ BRIDESMAIDS, ATTENDANTS AND PAGES

Cost and family politics usually come into play here. You can opt for none, an assortment of youngsters in your wake or a coterie of different ages and sizes.

Duties
- Looking gorgeous/photogenic
- Following you up the aisle
- Behaving themselves!

1 There's a considerable cost involved in outfitting a cast of bridesmaids and pages, although sometimes proud parents will chip in so their children can play a starring role. Like actors, brides know that working with small children means being upstaged – but the pleasure of seeing nieces, nephews or close friends' children decked out in wedding finery is invariably worth it.

2 Do choose at least one bridesmaid/page who is old and responsible enough to mind the others, particularly if they are under five. And remember that however charming they look, a teenie tantrum during the ceremony is a distinct possibility, so reconsider the idea if you aren't prepared to let your solemn procession be interrupted by a demonstration of toddler-power.

3 If you have older bridesmaids in the mix ('tweenies' or teens), find a compromise outfit or dress them differently but using a similar colour scheme. While two angelic six-year-olds may look delectable in pink flouncy dresses, their older and larger sisters may end up looking like oversized meringues and (quite justifiably) harbour bitter memories of the dress, the photos and your whole wedding day.

✧ USHERS

A perfect role for teenage brothers, cousins and friends, ushers are the first people many of your guests see, and they are particularly useful if you are hosting a large wedding.

Duties
- Greeting guests
- Getting everyone into (and out of) their seat
- Organising car parking/assisting with transport
- Helping the best man with general organisation

1 The great thing about ushers is that you can never have too many of them so this is a perfect way to give family and friends a defined role in your wedding without imposing too much of a burden on them. Pick at least one or two ushers who are older and more worldly-wise – they should be able to keep the others gainfully occupied and stop them looking like a gang of intimidating bouncers lurking outside the church (cigarettes, black shades, etc.). Get the best man to give each usher clearly proscribed 'meet and greet' duties – even particular guests to look out for – so they earn their buttonholes.

2 Once they get to the reception there is little left for them to do, although a good usher will keep a watchful eye on frail and unaccompanied guests, organise bags, coats and brollies and stay sober enough to help the best man keep the party running smoothly. There is no reason, by the way, why female ushers can't be appointed and this is a useful way of apportioning roles to friends and family who want to be involved.

✧ FAMILY ROLES

Your cast of attendants may be friends, but parents play a key role in making your wedding day complete. What duties you co-opt them for – beyond dressing up and acting as proud mum and dad – is up to you.

Bride's father

The bride's father can be a key player, walking her up the aisle and making one of the essential wedding speeches. It is perfectly acceptable for a guardian, stepfather or other close family member to step into the breach if there is no father of the bride. And some brides prefer to forgo the giving away side of the ceremony altogether and walk up the aisle alone.

Bride's mother

The bride's mother not only has to dress to impress, she may also be asked to give a speech at the wedding. Her key role is usually behind the scenes; but the amount of involvement she has in planning the wedding and keeping things running smoothly on the day depends on you.

Groom's father

Traditionally the groom's father had an easy ride. Dress the part, act as an official host and make merry. Many couples choose to equalise things – giving the father of the groom almost equal rights and responsibilities. For instance, he may get to make a speech at the reception and share planning/finance roles with the bride's parents.

Groom's mother

With no official role beyond supporting her son, dressing the part and standing in the official photos and reception line, the groom's mother traditionally took a secondary role to the bride's. But this is out of step with the way most weddings are planned and financed these days so it is a good idea to get her working as part of a team with the bride's mother. And if you break with tradition and let all the other parents get their turn on the podium it is politic to also let her make a speech.

Being fair to parents

It's easy – in the madness of organisation – to let one set of parents take over the reins and effectively side-line the other set. This could be because they are more eager to chip in with advice, because they have more time on their hands or because they live closer to you. Do make an effort to get them talking to each other directly – not using you as a conduit. The last thing you want on your wedding day is to be blamed for clashing outfits because you forgot to pass on the message that your mum was wearing pink. If the rapport isn't happening naturally, engineer it by organising moments where both sides come together. For instance, if the bride's mother is attending dress fittings or helping shop for shoes, the groom's mother could be invited along as well. And if the groom's father is going on the stag night, ask the bride's. The closer you get them

THE FINE ART OF DELEGATING

It can be tricky to hand over areas of responsibility to someone. After all, you reason, it's your day and only you know what's right. Er, wrong. Most weddings only happen because of teamwork so you need to let go. Here are some ideas.

Why delegate?

- It frees up time for the really important stuff (sleep, looking good on day, etc.).
- One brain can't possibly juggle full-time work, napkin colours, bridesmaids' dresses and a sit-down dinner for 100.
- Your parents/friends/relatives are dying to help, and will enjoy the wedding even more if they had a role in making it a success.

How to delegate

- Give people a thorough briefing of what you want and why you want it that way – as much information as possible.
- Now ask if they think this sounds a good idea (do listen to their response, but don't cave in if you don't agree) and let them gather ideas/estimates. Get updates along the line so you know that they haven't gone 'off message'.
- Hand over whole chunks of organisation. For instance, it's far more sensible for someone to deal with all flowers than just be given buttonholes.
- Don't breathe down their necks by ringing them every day. Every fortnight is fine unless it's wedding week, when you are entitled to ring every hour if it still hasn't been arranged.

What to delegate

- Flowers are an obvious choice. Add in table decorations as well to ensure the wedding looks colour schemed.
- Music – a good choice for a brother or sister. Let them source the DJ, approve the playlist (with your input unless you trust their taste implicitly) and badger him or her on the night if there's too little disco and too much Sinatra.
- Transport, because you can't be expected to think about bus and train times and memorise taxi numbers. Ideally, the best man should be involved in this one, but anyone who has a strategic mind, the ability to read timetables and the right attention to detail can be co-opted.
- Almost anything else that needs dedicated attention, including the reception organisation, menu, drinks ordering or marquee company. If you take a whole chunk of organisation off your shoulders it frees up time to think of the bigger picture. It also means you can relax because something is 'sorted'.

WHEN THINGS GO WRONG

Not everything your friends/family try to organise will be a masterpiece. However, unlike contractors they are doing you a favour so bite your tongue and try not to say something you will regret. Ask yourself if you gave them the right instructions in the first place or if you chose the right person to do the job. Stay calm, work with them and almost invariably the problem will be resolved successfully. Above all keep things in perspective and remember that your relationship is more important than one misunderstanding over your wedding day.

working together, the easier your day will become – and all future Christmases, family parties, etc.

✧ WITNESSES

A small but crucial role, your two witnesses sign on the line to say that you are truly married and their names appear forever on the record books.

This is one of those 'cameo' roles in a wedding that deserves some care and thought. Anyone asked to be a witness (and they must be over 18) has very little to do beyond witnessing the signing of the register with their signature, but it is an honour to be asked so could be a useful way of including someone you care about.

Some people choose both mothers, both fathers or a sibling from either side (and this is a nice gesture if you feel one of these groups hasn't had enough involvement). Other couples opt for close friends or ask their best man and chief bridesmaid. In a church wedding there are only two official witnesses but often a larger group of close family will be allowed to go with you to watch the register being signed. In a register office wedding the register is signed in front of all the guests.

✧ ROLES FOR OTHER FAMILY AND FRIENDS

There are plenty of other people you can include in the key preparations for the big day – from Aunt Bertha the talented chef to your old school-friend who just happens to be a concert violinist.

Here are some suggestions:

- **Cake** If you have a friend or relative who is a keen (and able) baker, then this is manna from heaven. Not only will you have a cake that means something more because it was lovingly prepared for you, you will also save money. It is appropriate to pay for all ingredients (a surprisingly hefty expense) and also to thank the person who made it in your speeches. A bouquet or other token would be a nice gesture.
- **Music** If a friend or family member is a talented amateur or professional singer/musician then this is a great opportunity to add live music to the wedding or reception. You will need to check that the wedding venue is happy to let them sing or play; violinists are usually easier to accommodate than pianists! Remember to thank them by including them in the order of service if you have one. And a formal thank you during the speeches is also a must.
- **Dressmaking/tailoring** You have hit the jackpot if someone you know is skilled enough to be entrusted with dresses, waistcoats or other wedding finery. Do be sure of their skills before you ask them (see The dresses came by train, below). Also check that they have the time/energy to invest in numerous fittings and alterations. It would be appropriate not only to thank them for their efforts during the speeches, but also to pay them something beyond the cost of materials. If they won't accept money, buy them an expensive and thoughtful gift for their house or garden.

True life stories: The dresses came by train

When Rose was planning her wedding outfits she decided to approach her good friend and aspiring fashion designer Lynn. She loved the initial designs and Lynn was enthusiastic during the early stages of the work, taking them to a wholesale fabric merchant to choose fine silks, organising fittings for Rose and her three bridesmaids and suggesting elegant accessories to make their outfits complete. But as the months rolled on it became more difficult for Lynn to manage the commitment as she had accepted another job. Add to that the fact that the bride and one of the bridesmaids were losing weight and it became a nightmare of organisation. The night before the wedding, Lynn was up all night finishing off seams and sewing on buttons. 'It was about as nightmarish as it could get,' says Rose. 'On the morning of my wedding my sister had to cancel her hair appointment and drive down to the station to pick up the dresses. They arrived on the 7.47am train, accompanied by an exhausted looking Lynn. The dresses looked lovely but, frankly, it wasn't worth the stress.'

PRE-WEDDING PARTIES

The party before the party is as restrained or as outlandish as you make it. Some couples opt for wild stag and hen weekends, others reject the tradition as outdated or prefer to host a joint gathering. Whatever you choose, here are some guidelines.

✧ THE STAG NIGHT

For some grooms the stag night has become almost more of a rite of passage than the wedding itself. By tradition it was held the night before the wedding – something almost all couples avoid these days (the dangers are too obvious to need describing). It can take place a week or several months before the main event and many celebrations have grown into two- or three-night holidays. Before you go for broke here are some pointers:

• **Cost** Although the groom used to finance the stag night, this is not normally how it works these days (particularly if you are planning a weekend away). Most guests will be more than happy to contribute, although that means they also have a say in the location and price tag.

• **Location** Low-cost flights and the promise of cheap beer and the company of strangers have inspired stag parties to travel further. This requires careful planning and the best man is usually also chief organiser and 'master of ceremonies'.

• **Jokes** Grooms expect a variety of tricks of the low and cheap variety to be played on them. It is worth ensuring your best man knows how far you are prepared to laugh along with this. If there's a danger he will allow things to go too far then you might want to reconsider his role as organiser.

- **Drunkenness and debauchery** The former is allowed, the latter is neither safe nor sensible. While 'no cameras' and other rules ensure the groom won't be immortalised at his lowest point, it is simply not worth organising anything that could jeopardise the wedding or shatter the bride-to-be's faith in both her groom and his entire circle of male friends.

- **Adrenaline** A popular alternative to the all-you-can-drink weekend, these are usually action and adventure sessions, from go-karting and tank driving to the chance to parachute, play shoot-'em-up games or go on every scary ride at a theme park. Remember that the costs of these activities can equal – or surpass – a cheap flight to Europe, although you might decide it's worth the expense because it's a more memorable and photographable activity than a pub-crawl.

CAN THEY AFFORD IT?

If you choose a stag night in an exotic or expensive location then you may find close friends have to drop out of the party because they can't afford the time or money. The chance to go wild in Vilnius needs to be balanced against the fact that people you want to share the experience with won't be there. If it is one or two people (students, younger brothers) then it may be worth getting the rest of the party to chip in a little bit more, or you could agree to pay their way on your own account.

True life stories: Big bill in Barcelona

One rarely reported hazard of being in a stag party is that restaurant and bar owners who are willing to let you party with them may also take a few liberties with the bill. For John it was a sobering night. He and his friends were weekending in Barcelona and after hitting the bars they decided to look for something to eat. 'There were about 20 of us in varying stages of drunkenness. We stopped to look at the menu outside a nice looking but empty restaurant and the owner came outside to invite us in. It was impossible to order for such a large group so he said he would serve us with a mixture of "specialities",' says John. What the canny restaurateur had worked out was that he could get rid of all the unsold fish and shellfish in the fridges of his empty restaurant. John takes up the story, 'All these huge dishes of prawns and mussels kept arriving – I don't even like seafood! Eventually we called a halt but the bill cost more than our flights and not one of us had enough Spanish to argue our case. We had a very sober and poverty-stricken final day.'

DID YOU KNOW...? BEWARE THE STAG NIGHT BAN

The very words 'stag party' can be enough to ensure you are barred from the hotel/bar/restaurant/club of your choice, so unless you are sure your group is going to behave with sobriety and discretion it is worth being upfront about the nature of your party and ringing ahead to check or make a confirmed booking. Some establishments are happy to take your money, others have a blanket ban on large posses of unaccompanied men. This can seem unfair in an era when many bar managers quietly admit it's the hens that should truly be feared, but your reputation precedes you.

✧ THE HEN NIGHT

Equality can mean more drinking and more rowdiness than the men, as anyone who has seen a group of hens on a night out can testify. But there are more diverse and sedate options if you don't fancy dressing up in a tiara for the evening or hitting the dance floor for a last-night-of-freedom celebration. Here are some pointers:

- **Cost** The hen night is a more flexible tradition and can involve a close group of female family and friends or a much larger cast of players. Costs are invariably shared, although you may find that family and friends pay for the hen's meal/entertainment.
- **Location** Equality rules, so it could be a weekend away or an adrenaline-packed adventure just like the boys. More low-key alternatives include smart restaurants, a night at a pub/club or a

party at a friend's house. The chief bridesmaid (if you have one) may organise the event, but some brides-to-be prefer to take control.

- **Drunkenness and debauchery** The inner 'ladette' tends to emerge as the night wears on, but be particularly cautious if you are in a foreign or unfamiliar city, particularly if there are different conventions on acceptable dress that could lead to misunderstandings with the local males or unwanted attention from the police. As far as debauchery goes, the same rules apply as for stag nights, so ensure the organiser keeps it within acceptable bounds.
- **Gifts** In the USA, it is customary for the hen to be plied with gifts at her 'wedding shower' and it's a tradition that is finding favour here. Gifts can be sensible or jokey, depending on the sort of evening you are having. Get someone to take charge of them for you, or plan to start the night in someone's home so you can leave them there.
- **Pampering** An alternative way to spend your money and time, pampering afternoons or weekends make sense if you have a mixed party (e.g. mothers) or you just prefer the idea of detoxing and de-stressing to a lager marathon. Health farms and clubs offer package deals, or you could head to an exotic spa for the ultimate pre-wedding prep session.

HENS PLAY SAFE

While it may feel like equality rules OK, a crowd of drunken hens can become an easy target for predatory males. It's important to stick together – nominate someone to count you in and out of bars and clubs. Also ensure that you pre-arrange transport home at the end of the evening, particularly if you are going back to your respective homes. Licensed taxis (never unlicensed cabs) should be booked at the start of the evening and no one should journey home alone on public transport. Never abandon anyone in a bar or club, particularly if you think they are the worse for wear.

✧ ALTERNATIVE IDEAS

It doesn't have to be a segregated drinking contest – particularly if you don't feel you are losing your 'freedom' by getting married. Here are other suggestions for organising a party.

- **Joint weekend** This can be a cost-effective way of combining the stag/hen weekends since everyone gets to share a double room with their partner/friend. Popular options include country house hotels and rented houses and you can add on activities to be undertaken jointly or in male/female groups – for instance golf, horse riding and leisure centre/pampering activities.

- **Restaurant** The best solution if you want to include parents/older relatives in your pre-wedding party but don't feel a wild stag or hen night is appropriate. You can arrange a mixed party or have separate evenings for the male/female guests. If stag and hens do go their separate ways, it's a nice touch if they can come together at the beginning or end of the evening.

- **Drinks party** Both the simplest to organise and the cheapest way to mark the impending wedding (particularly if you host it at home), this mixes male and female partygoers for a relaxed drink. Guests can pay their own way or bring a bottle, though if you can afford it, start the evening off with a welcome drink. Jugs of Pimm's, or mulled wine in winter, will get the evening off to a lively start.

NOT IN FRONT OF THE PARENTS

You may want your parent there on your stag/hen night or he or she may express a wish to come. However it gets decided, this should definitely have an impact on the shape of your evening. Only you know the fine line that should never be crossed, so brief your friends on the sort of behaviour that will take things too far. If there's a danger they may see you in an unfamiliar and unpleasant light, then it's better to leave mum or dad off the guest list and organise a separate and more restrained event for them and your older relatives. (See Alternative ideas, above.)

TROUBLESHOOTING

✧ HOW TO SAVE THE DAY IF YOU CAUSE OFFENCE

'My brother is offended that I didn't make him my best man. I tried to explain that I felt obliged to choose my best friend (I was his best man) but now my brother is being very distant and I think my mother is also upset about my choice.'

With weddings, it is not a case of *if* you offend someone but *when*. The first thing you have to do is step away from the situation and ask yourself whose wedding it is? Yours is the answer and that means you have to make your own decisions. Once you've stopped feeling guilty you can start to bring people round to your point of view.

1 Try inviting your brother out to the pub/golf course or wherever it is you two normally meet up. No one else should be invited. Don't raise the topic immediately – wait until you've both chatted for a bit – but then be direct about why you made the choice you did. Ask him if he can understand the situation from your point of view and explain to him how important it is that he be alongside you on your big day.

2 See if you can find your brother some other important role in the whole affair: chief usher, reception party organiser, stag night supremo… And if you can bear the double humiliation of your early childhood/teenage gaffes being exposed to the world perhaps you can ask him to make a short speech at the reception before your best man.

3 Once your brother is on side your mother should calm down. If not, it may be because she feels one of her children is being 'left out' (fairness is a typical parental angst). Enlist the support of your brother – even go and see your mother together. Again, you need to explain simply and honestly why you made the decision you did. Be patient but firm and eventually you should win her round to your point of view.

✧ REFUSING AN OFFER OF HELP

'My future mother-in-law is a keen florist and has offered her services with the flowers. The trouble is I don't like her taste.'

This is a tricky one and you have to walk a diplomatic tightrope since she has been good enough to offer. Be very careful not to turn a small issue into a big one by rejecting her offer out of hand. Here are some options.

1 Be honest – not brutally so – by telling her you have very specific plans for your flowers and you are not sure she will agree with your taste (this neatly turns it round so you are the one with the questionable judgement). Show her some examples of the sort of arrangements you were thinking of and even work by a florist you admire. Remember to thank her for being kind enough to offer her services.

2 Tell her you have already provisionally lined someone up for the flowers (an allowable white lie) but then ask her to help you organise something else. Obviously if you don't like her taste you don't want to let her loose on the table-settings, but you could get her involved in something organisational or ask her to accompany you to planning meetings with caterers or venue.

3 If you think she will take it in the right spirit, let her take on the flowers but under your firm guidance. This will only work if she is competent enough to change her flower arranging style and also willing to listen to your ideas. It could take some time and diplomacy but the bonus is you will get your flowers arranged with love and dedication (and for less money).

✧ RESOLVING AN ARGUMENT

'My best friend agreed to be my bridesmaid but now she has threatened to back out because she says she hates the dress I've chosen for her. I'm really upset and the argument is threatening to put a dampener on the day.'

It's a shame that you've come to blows on this one and that your best friend let it go this far. But a grown woman has been given a 'uniform' she doesn't like and we all remember how that felt from our schooldays. You need to try and salvage the situation and maybe listen to her opinion.

1 The first question to ask is why she doesn't like the dress. Does it make her feel self-conscious or fat? Perhaps it's the colour, or the design is too revealing. None of us wants to feel we look stupid. You need to get her input before you can remedy the situation – and perhaps accept a compromise if you want her as your bridesmaid.

2 If the dress is still on the drawing board or in the bridal shop then you have time to come up with an alternative design. Let her put forward suggestions by showing you dresses she feels comfortable in or colours that work for her. You don't want to change your wedding outfit just to suit her, but you should be able to tone down the offending colour or come up with a style she finds more flattering.

3 If the dress is already made then you have more limited options, but it could still be possible to adapt it or introduce an addition (a cardigan or jacket) that will make her feel comfortable. Talk your options through with her and with the wedding shop/designer and see what is possible in the time you have left.

4 Don't let this become an all-consuming problem; it is just one facet of your day. If you can't resolve the problems with your best friend, you need to forget her as a bridesmaid and focus on having a happy wedding. Ensure your friend is still invited as a guest.

CHAPTER 4

PAPERWORK & PRACTICALITIES

Some wedding formalities are essential and others are up to you. It helps to know the traditional rules, even if you choose to word your invitation differently or forget about making a newspaper announcement.

In this chapter you'll find out the options for public and private announcements of your marriage. There's also guidance on the protocol for gift lists and advice on choosing (and vetting) your suppliers and handling donations and tips. The at-a-glance planning calendar at the end of the chapter gives essential pointers on what to do – and when – in the run up to your wedding.

ANNOUNCING YOUR WEDDING

Whatever traditions you do abandon, once you have satisfied the church or register office that you are eligible to marry, you must make a public announcement that you are going to get married. This is a legal requirement, since it gives someone the chance to object (don't worry, they can only do this if you are already married or too young/too closely related). Although it sounds rather solemn and grown-up, in practise it is just a formality that your church or register office will handle on your behalf.

✧ BANNS

For Anglican (Church of England and Wales) weddings, banns are the usual method of publicising the marriage. This tradition dates back over 800 years and the minister is legally allowed to act as registrar. The banns are a short statement detailing the names of the parties being married and they are read out in the parish where the couple are to be married on three Sundays before the wedding (usually three consecutive ones although legally they must be done in the three months leading up to the wedding). It is not obligatory to attend when they are read out, but many couples like to be there and the minister will appreciate your presence. If one or both of you lives in another parish, the banns will also be read in that church and you need to contact the minister to arrange this. Banns are included in the cost of the church wedding.

✧ GIVING NOTICE

For civil weddings in a register office or approved wedding venue, and for services in all other religious buildings, you have to give notice at your local register office that you are to be married. If you live in different districts you will each have to apply to your respective register office. Like the banns, this is a public announcement, except in this case it is displayed on a notice board at the register office for 15 clear days. It contains your full name, age, address, occupation, nationality and intended wedding venue. Once issued, the notice is valid for 12 months. Don't forget that if you intend to marry at a different register office from where both of you live you will also have to notify the registrar in that district so they can book someone to attend your wedding.

DID YOU KNOW...? WHAT IT COSTS

- Fees for Church of England and Wales weddings are £170–250 including the banns. They do not include extras such as lighting, choirs, etc. so remember to discuss these with the minister.
- For Church of Scotland weddings there is no official fee, but you may be asked to pay a contribution for heating, lighting, organist, etc. so you need to speak to the minister of the church where you want to marry.
- Fees for a civil wedding at a register office are £40 and you pay an additional £60 (£30 each) to give notice that you will be married.
- Fees for a civil wedding at an approved wedding venue are set by your local authority, but will include the cost of attendance by the superintendent registrar and registrar. You also have to pay £60 to give notice and probably pay an additional fee to the wedding venue.
- For a religious ceremony at a building other than a church of the Church of England and Wales, costs depend on whether you are married by an 'authorised person' (this is a someone officially allowed to conduct marriage ceremonies). If not, you pay £47 for the registrar's attendance. You will also pay £60 to give notice and may be liable for additional costs to the church or other religious building.
- Once you've done it you can prove it! Marriage certificates cost a very reasonable £3.50.

✧ NEWSPAPER ANNOUNCEMENTS

These are a traditional way of telling the wider world that you are about to be hitched and there is a fairly standard wording – depending on the newspaper – for making this news public. In many cases the announcement is of far more importance to the parents of the couple than the couple themselves. Formal wording is making way for more personal language – particularly in local papers – so check the publication where you want to place your advert to get inspiration. Here are three examples:

National newspaper

The engagement is announced between Thomas, eldest son of
Mr and Mrs Fred Green of Farnborough, Surrey, and Jane Anne,
youngest daughter of Mr and Mrs John Brown of Kingston,
Surrey.

Local newspaper

Mr and Mrs John Brown of Kingston, Surrey are delighted to
announce the engagement of their daughter Jane to Thomas, son of
Mr and Mrs Fred Green.

Alternative local newspaper

Jane Brown and Thomas Green of Kingston, Surrey are delighted
to announce their engagement.

✧ WEDDING INVITATIONS

You can be as formal or informal as you like with wedding
invitations. The key thing to remember is that these set the tone of
your big day and provide a useful clue for guests about what to
wear and (more importantly) what to expect. However creative or
casual you choose to be with wording, there are some basics you
must include within your invitation. Leave them out at your peril –
you'll be barraged with phone calls or risk getting married minus
half your invited guests.

Essentials to include
- Your name and your partner's name
- Guest's name (just in case your invitation is delivered to a
  complete stranger who decides to turn up anyway!)
- Venue (be specific about village/area – particularly if it's a church)
- Date
- Time (give the real time, rather than building in slack for tardy
  friends)
- Reception venue
- RSVP information

Formal invitations

Formal invitations follow a tried and trusted formula (see Example 1) that dates back to the days when brides were literally 'given away' by their families. The formality may seem a bit dated but it's a style that most recipients understand as a sign that you're having 'the works'. If this is the format you decide on but it seems a bit distant, you can always personalise the cards by attaching a short handwritten note or writing on the invitation itself ('can't wait to see you' or 'getting nervous already' should break the ice). Also remember that you don't have to go for an ornate or old-world script – often setting a formal invitation in a more contemporary typeface makes it seem more friendly (see Choosing typefaces, page 69).

EXAMPLE 1

Mr & Mrs John Brown

request the pleasure of the company of

_____ (guest's name here)

at the marriage of their daughter
Jane Anne
to
Mr Thomas Green
at St Mary's Church
London, SW18
On Saturday 1 March
at 4pm
and afterwards at a reception at
The Angel Hotel, Kingston

RSVP
The Rookery
16 Long Lane
Kingston
KT16 4QS

DIVORCED OR DECEASED

The wording of a formal invitation can be altered to accommodate family circumstances. The four examples below show you alternative ways of wording a formal invitation to suit different family set-ups. The key point to remember is that the wedding hosts always go at the top of the invitation.

Divorced
Mr John Brown and Mrs Eileen Brown

Divorced and remarried parents as joint hosts
Mr John Brown and Mrs David Cooper

Deceased parent
Mrs John Brown
Requests the pleasure of the company of
_____ (guest's name here)
at the marriage of Jane Brown
daughter of the late Mr John Brown

Parent and step-parent as joint hosts
Mr and Mrs John Brown
Request the pleasure of the company of
_____ (guest's name here)
at the marriage of Jane Brown
daughter of the late Eileen Brown

69

Choosing Typefaces

The typeface you choose sets the tone almost as much as the language you use.

- *Scrolls and italicised typefaces have a more formal and traditional feel.*
- A simple font looks more friendly and contemporary.

Look at a variety of samples so you can compare typefaces. Do avoid mixing and matching typefaces or going for a wildly ornate script – the first approach looks amateurish and the second will be impossible for people with anything less than 20/20 vision to read.

Informal invitations

Many couples choose to send out their own invitations. This avoids the stuffiness that can sometimes creep into formal wedding invitations and also gives scope to use more contemporary and personal language. This is also the best option if you are marrying for the second time. The choice of style and format is really up to you, but here is a typical invitation to use as a starting point. You will note that all the essentials are still listed and in the same order as for a formal invitation.

EXAMPLE 2

Jane Brown & Thomas Green
invite _____ (guest's name here)
to celebrate their marriage
at St Mary's Church
London, SW18
On Saturday 1 March
at 4pm
Followed by a party
at The Angel Hotel, Kingston

RSVP
12a Orchard Close
London
SW18 4LE

Evening-only invitations

If some guests are invited to the evening party but not the service itself you need to prepare separate invitations for them. The wording is very straightforward so follow the style of your main invitation but give the new time and venue. It's also a good idea to state that this is the party only ('evening reception' if you want to be formal) and not the service so these guests can leave the hats and morning suits at home. It goes without saying that you need to keep split guest lists and their respective invitations entirely separate – in separate rooms if possible – as your aged aunts and uncles may never forgive you if they experience the disco but miss out on the church.

Be specific on names

Do remember to include the names of everyone who is invited; don't just assume that people will know to bring their partner or children. Of course, if you leave off names for a reason – say because children aren't invited – you cannot assume everyone will follow your instructions to the letter. Be prepared to conjure up a few extra chairs on the day if someone unexpected turns up.

What else to include

Your smart white invitation cards give the essential information and will look lovely on the mantelpiece, but you can help your guests enormously by sending an accompanying fact sheet. Not only is this going to save you time in fielding phone calls and emails, it also helps your guests feel you want their presence and have gone the extra mile for them. Keep the tone brief but friendly and include the following essentials:

- Directions to wedding venue (road plus rail/bus)
- Directions to reception venue (if different)
- Taxi numbers (two or three reputable local firms)
- Special information such as where to park (essential if you have 70 cars turning up at a tiny village church or a busy city centre register office)
- Contact details for three or four surrounding inns/hotels (include a budget option alongside more expensive choices)

Many of your guests will be making a long journey and going to considerable expense, so as a courtesy you may want to call the inns/hotels before you list them to see if you can negotiate a discount. Even if they only offer a nominal reduction on their room rate it shows additional thought on your part and makes it more likely your guests will round off a happy event with new-found friends in the hotel bar. If you are marrying somewhere off the beaten track, you might also want to include a line at the bottom of the fact sheet suggesting that if people are stuck for transport they contact you. Perhaps you can link them up with other guests for a lift or help out by sending a taxi/driver to meet them from the train or bus station. Some couples lay on a minibus or coach, which can be a practical and cost-efficient way to ferry guests.

THE TRICKY BUSINESS OF GIFT LISTS

Guests invariably want to bring you gifts, but do you want the presents they bring? The old joke about weddings being marked by an abundance of unwanted toasters may not happen in real life (surely no one would dare just turn up with one?) but without some direction from you there is a fair chance you will be making many trips to the charity shop or putting ornaments out on display only when you are expecting visits from the givers. So gift lists are a marvellous idea. However, many people still feel uncomfortable advertising the fact they have got one.

DID YOU KNOW...? THE ORIGINS OF GIFT LISTS

We may see them as a chance to get our friends to spend, spend, spend, but gift lists were originally a way of ensuring the lovestruck young couple had the bare essentials for setting up their new life together. Family and friends would choose key components to help fill their bare and barely affordable new home, and generally focused on the strictly practical such as bed linen, kitchen pans and furniture.

✧ TWO SCHOOLS OF THOUGHT

There are two entirely different ways of handling your gift list; the choice you make depends on your own preference and the attitude of your guests.

Old school says you should not mention your gift list on any invitations or accompanying literature you send out to your guests. The merest mention makes you grasping. It is, however, acceptable when asked to say that you have a gift list and then provide more information.

Progressive school says this is frankly outdated because almost all your guests will be hounding you for details so you can save time and phone calls by mentioning it on your invitation. If you do go for this option it is a good idea not to appear badgering and some couples put in a line saying 'Please don't feel you have to bring us anything, but if you do wish to buy a gift our list is at ____ (name of company, contact details/website, gift list number or reference code).'

✦ HOW TO SET UP A GIFT LIST

You can choose from online stores, department stores or mail order companies – the decision is yours. But you will need to register in advance. In some instances this means going in to register, even taking a trip round the store armed with a scan gun so you can mark all the items you would like on your gift list. In others you can go through all the formalities online. In almost all cases the service is free (the store stands to make a lot of money from you).

✦ HOW TO PICK YOUR GIFT LIST PROVIDER

- **Location of store** Can nearly all your guests get to a branch if they want to pick your present in person?
- **Quality of service** Does the store/gift list have a phone ordering service with helpful operators and no long queues? Online-only ordering is fine for your friends who are computer literate, but possibly not such a good idea for elderly relatives.
- **Scope of gifts** The deciding factor. You not only want a good range of products, but a good range of price points.
- **Efficiency/delivery** You need to know that all orders will be processed properly and that gifts will be delivered at a time to suit you. Check if you have to pay for delivery.

Tips for creating your gift list

This may sound like your chance to do a trolley dash round your favourite store, but it's actually harder to compile than you might imagine. Here are some points to watch out for:

- First and most essentially, go for a wide range of price points and include plenty of options under £20. Some people may buy you more than one cheaper item, but at least this shows you are not expecting the earth. Unless all your friends are in the millionaire bracket you should set an upper limit for individual items of £100.
- Don't decide that this is the moment to complete your first wildly expensive dinner service. While a single dinner plate costing £50 might be gratefully received, the giver will know what you are up to and probably resent such a lavish use of their money.
- Taking account of the above, do be imaginative. This is your excuse to include things that you might not be able to justify buying for yourself. Those Egyptian cotton bathrobes or gorgeous designer wine glasses are pleasurable luxuries that people will enjoy choosing, because they are going to be memorable to you.
- If you are setting up home for the first time and desperately need practical gifts (including that toaster) then people will understand this and be happy to give you this type of gift. Do spare them the more gruesome practicalities though – no one wants to be remembered for giving you a toilet brush.
- Don't just give people the gift list option. Some people might prefer to give you gift vouchers – ensure the store where you have your list makes this clear when people contact them.

✧ ALTERNATIVE GIFT IDEAS

It could be that you don't need anything for your home or you would prefer a different style of gift. Here are ideas for something different.

- **DIY store/garden centre vouchers** If you are renovating a wreck or landscaping that bare patch of mud out back then these can be a great help to you, and your guests will appreciate helping out in your hour of need. To thank them for their generosity send updates showing the improvements to your house and garden.

- **Travel vouchers** A popular idea for couples who plan the honeymoon of all honeymoons or who intend to go travelling for a longer period after the wedding. A postcard from some exotic destination is the very least they should expect in thanks!
- **Gifts to charity** This is an option for the couple who have everything, or who have a particular cause they wish to support. Don't be too 'holier than thou' about it though and ensure this is a cause that no one can disagree with.

True life stories: Adding style to a world trip

Alexis and Dimitri knew they wanted to go travelling in India straight after their wedding so their honeymoon budget was stretched. They had already paid for flights and essentials, but as an alternative to the conventional wedding list they decided to ask guests to add on 'treats' to their journey. 'We were roughing it for most of the time so decided it would be a nice idea to let wedding guests buy us the luxuries. Rather than ask them to donate money with no idea what it would be spent on we broke the gift list down under individual headings. We included things like "A Night In A Floating Palace" and "A Train Ride Through Rajasthan"' says Alexis. The idea worked brilliantly because although none of these items was that horrendously expensive individually, together they made this the trip of a lifetime. Everyone who had donated something was remembered with a postcard from that precise location.

DID YOU KNOW...? DIFFERENT TRADITIONS

At some Greek and Philippine weddings, guests pin cash onto the bride's dress as a gift to the couple. The lucky bride might have her outfit completely covered with crisp banknotes.

In India the traditional gift is jewellery for the bride; relatives and friends spend a small fortune so she is awash with gold by the time of her wedding.

CHOOSING & VETTING SUPPLIERS

You may be a quantity surveyor or management accountant in your working life, but even the most scrupulous of us can forget some basic rules in the romance (and panic) of wedding organisation. You need to ensure that everyone who is being paid to contribute to your day will deliver as promised. Here are six general guidelines.

- **Ask for estimates/quotes (and know the difference)** Always get an idea of costs before you start. Ask if the costing is an estimate or a fixed quote. The first is a ballpark figure that may alter, the second is an agreed price that can't be altered without approval from you. Where possible, go back to suppliers after you have agreed to an estimate and ask them to create a more detailed and accurate costing.

- **Check if VAT is included** It is all too easy to think a price looks reasonable and then realise you have to pay an additional 17.5 per cent – not such a bargain.

- **Ask for references/testimonials** This is added security for you because it shows that the company didn't start trading last week. What is more, by asking for details of previous clients you have the chance to check up on the service they have provided in the past.

- **Never pay everything up front** Deposits vary hugely, but in almost all instances you should not be paying anything approaching the full fee unless you have received the contracted

ONE-STOP WEDDING SHOPPING

If you have too much to plan and too little free time, go to a wedding fair where you can select all your suppliers on one day. These are held around the country – check your local press or national bridal magazines for details. The best of them bring together just about every detail you can imagine (plus many you hadn't even thought of) for your big party. You will be able to see and vet the work of caterers, florists, dress designers and drinks companies. There are usually plenty of potential wedding venues in attendance and many fairs also include an area devoted to honeymoon destinations.

BUDGET FOR CONTINGENCIES

Wedding suppliers are very good at getting people to part with more money than they had originally budgeted for. So be on the look out for marketing tricks of the trade such as silver, gold and diamond wedding plans (who wants to be measly silver when they could be diamond?). Manage your a budget like a miser and learn the art of saying 'No' to bigger and better suggestions and you will stop your finances escalating out of control. Do, however, ensure you have a reserve fund – 10 to 15 per cent is typical – so you can sort out problems or manage unexpected overspends. Keep this money in a separate account so you won't be tempted to touch it unless you really need it. One good way to ring-fence the cash is to promise yourselves another exciting use for it after the wedding – perhaps a second great holiday a year down the line. That way you are demonstrating cost control and giving yourselves something to look forward to.

service – it leaves you in a very weak bargaining position if your contractor fails to deliver to your satisfaction. Check the deposit at the time of booking and ensure you receive a proper receipt for anything you pay in advance of your wedding.

- **Ask questions in writing** Verbal agreements won't stand up if you have a dispute with a contractor so start a paper trail by putting agreements in writing. So if you understand that your marquee company will have a person on site, put that in your next letter to them. Ensure you detail any extras their salesperson agreed, particularly if they are not included in general brochures/literature. Raise questions if there is anything you are unsure about and ensure they come back to you in writing to confirm things.

- **Check the small print** Unless you are going through a 'one stop' wedding service there may be a variety of contractors on site and this can be one of your biggest headaches. Read the small print to ensure that you don't get caught out. In particular check what is and isn't allowed by your wedding venue. It could be something minor (venue doesn't allow red wine) or something major (venue insists music stops at 9pm) but either way you need to know about it in advance.

✧ WHEN PLANS GO AWRY

Almost no wedding runs like the well oiled machine you had designed, but the first rule is: don't panic. You need to stay calm. You also need to do some clear and rational thinking so you can sort things out.

If the problem arises before the big day, call in the cavalry by enlisting the support of friends/family or work colleagues. Even major crises such as the venue pulling out have a solution and group research is much more likely to be successful. Everyone knows someone and that network of connections could provide a miracle (e.g. charming country house hotel that doesn't have a wedding on the same day). It definitely helps if you have some cash to spend on the problem, so if you are the worrying type take out wedding insurance (see Consider wedding insurance, below).

If it's a problem on the day itself then your options are more limited. But you have to distinguish between the biggies (non-arrival of caterer) and the merely irritating (non-arrival of chocolate fountain). The reality is that almost all issues will not be noticed by your guests, provided they have something to drink. They don't know your day was perfectly planned down to the tiniest canapé. Even if they do notice they will be understanding, so

CONSIDER WEDDING INSURANCE

Insurance can buy you peace of mind – and get you out of trouble if the marquee company goes bust or your outfit is ruined two weeks ahead of the big day. Cover can be as comprehensive or limited as you like but typically costs from around £50. Look for a policy that includes failure of suppliers, wedding/reception cancellation, loss or damage of gifts, personal liability/accident and legal expenses. Remember that policies won't cover you for wedding cancellation unless there is a cast-iron reason such as illness or a family bereavement (cold feet isn't one of them). You should definitely take out insurance if you plan to get married abroad – most overseas wedding specialists will offer this as part of your wedding package. Check the cover – and the exclusion clauses – very carefully.

relax and enjoy the wedding party for what it is (rather than what it should have been). And don't put your own dampener on the day by telling everyone what has gone wrong.

True life stories: The wedding dress disaster

When Kat was shopping for wedding dresses she was horrified by the costs of almost everything she liked. On her third outing a very helpful shop assistant whispered that she was actually a bridal designer and could make a similar outfit for a third of the cost. Kat thought this sounded a great idea and since the woman lived close to her she went for a fitting. Three months down the line she had paid the 'designer' around half the cost of the dress but it became impossible to contact her to arrange fittings. And when she finally got to see her she was horrified by the dress. 'She hadn't made it in the material I asked for,' says Kat. 'Not only that but seams were wonky and it didn't fit me properly at all.' With just two months to go before her wedding Kat was finally forced to abandon the dress and its maker altogether and go shopping for a ready-to-wear outfit. 'I was embarrassed more than anything else. Why would anyone trust a person who was touting for her own business while working for another employer? I finally found a dress I loved, but in the end, I'd paid double.'

True life stories: My florist damaged the church

Bernadette and Patrick were thrilled that they received permission to marry in their city's historic cathedral and Patrick's mother took charge of the flowers by booking a talented local florist she knew. The flowers looked spectacular but after they returned from honeymoon the cathedral office contacted them to say that there had been some damage to the building. 'We couldn't believe it but the florist had secured some of the flowers to the stonework by hammering in nails. We felt awful because we were effectively responsible for the damage,' says Patrick. The florist hadn't thought to contact the cathedral office before she got her hammer out and the resulting restoration had to be undertaken by specialist stonemasons. 'In the end it wasn't as bad as we had imagined, but we felt duty bound to pay for the renovation work,' says Bernadette. 'The worst thing about it was that the florist couldn't understand why anyone would get upset about her banging a few holes into a medieval pillar.'

DONATIONS, GIFTS & TIPS

Don't get caught out when you draw up your wedding finances –
there will be a long list of extras you may be asked (or feel
obliged) to add on to your costs. Here are things you may need
to budget for.

- **Church/religious building donation** This is implied or asked for
directly by many places when you book a wedding. Ask them to
give you an idea of what they expect if you are in any doubt, but
£100–150 might be typical.
- **Reception venue** If you hold your reception in a village hall,
scout hut or farmer's field you have probably saved on hire costs,
but might be asked (or feel it appropriate) to give something back
in the way of a donation. Budget for £50–100.
- **Car parking** If you get permission for guests to park their cars in
a village hall or school car park it is usual to give a donation.
Budget for up to £50.
- **Bridesmaids/pages gifts** These don't have to be wildly expensive
but should be mementos they can keep. Jewellery or dolls might
be appropriate for female attendants, books or a wristwatch for
male attendants. Budget for £20–25 per attendant.
- **Best man gift** Not essential but often couples choose to mark the
day with something the best man can keep, such as a pair of
cufflinks. Budget for £30–40.
- **Parents and helpers gifts** Flowers are the most common gift for
parents – a joint gift but given to the mothers of the bride and
groom. You may also want to arrange bouquets for anyone who
offered additional help above and beyond the call of duty. Budget
for £20–25 per bouquet.
- **Wedding reception/bar staff** Tips are often given to the staff
who serve your guests (with the proviso that you must be happy
with the service) and the best man takes charge of this, using
your cash. The amount you give depends on the number of staff
and whether or not they have a kitty. Budget for £50–100.
- **Taxis** Keep cash in reserve in case you need to tip cab drivers to
persuade them to take a worse-for-wear guest home. About

£5–10 per cab should do it, depending on how bad the guest is. Of course you may also have to pay the guest's fare.

CHANGING NAMES

Legally, women don't have to take their husband's surname, so there is no pressure to get this organised in the run up to the wedding, or even decide before you marry. The one crucial detail to watch is passports – if you have booked honeymoon tickets in your married names you will need to ensure that your passport matches flight details. The UK Passport Agency can arrange an amendment up to three months before your marriage. Bear in mind you won't be able to travel until you are married if you choose this option.

Here are other organisations that may need to be notified if you are making a change. Normally they will accept a photocopy of your marriage certificate.

- DVLA – driving licence, car registration
- Insurer – car/household/life/travel
- Pension provider
- Bank
- Building society
- Credit card companies
- Registrars of shares
- Work (accounts department)
- Inland Revenue
- DSS – National Insurance
- Medical – GP/dentist
- Local authority – electoral register, council tax
- HM Land Registry – home
- Utilities – gas/electricity/water/phone/mobile phone
- TV Licensing office

Double barrelling your name

Many couples choose to take on both names once they are married. This is not something that can be done automatically on your marriage certificate but you can apply for a name change by Deed Poll. Currently you pay £39 per person (£34 if you order online), but if you apply at the same time as a couple it costs £29 (£24 online). There is no need to involve solicitors and all financial institutions/government bodies will accept your Deed Poll as proof of your new identity. If you do this after the wedding then your marriage certificate cannot be amended. For this reason, the UK Deed Poll Service recommends that if you want your marriage certificate to show your new identity, the man should apply in advance of the wedding. That way his wife automatically takes on a new double-barrelled identity and doesn't have to apply for a change of name by Deed Poll. You will need to apply at least two weeks before the wedding.

What name to choose

It is up to you which name goes first, although traditionally the husband's name would go last. Fine in principle, but if it looks and sounds wrong then many couples decide to reverse the name. You can also decide whether or not to include a hyphen. Some couples decide to do things differently and the woman changes her name so that her maiden surname becomes, in effect, a first name (e.g. Jane Anne becomes Jane Anne Brown) and then tacks on her new surname (e.g. Green, to become Jane Anne Brown Green) once she is married. Just remember that the version you write on the application form will be binding – unless you go through the whole Deed Poll process again.

✧ KEEPING YOUR PROFESSIONAL NAME

You may have spent years building up your professional reputation and it can be hard to let go of the name people recognise, even if you decide to take on your husband's name after marriage. Just as female actors often keep a 'stage name', many women continue to be known by their maiden name in their working life. If you choose this option it is a good idea to let your employer know what you intend to do – most will be relaxed about this – although if your bank details have changed they will need to amend their 'official' records to ensure your salary goes into the right account and the Tax Office knows how to find you.

✧ BEWARE OF CHEAP NAME CHANGES

There are various other ways of changing your name – including going through a solicitor – but most will cost you more. Be cautious about signing up for a suspiciously cheap internet offer. Some are not worth the paper they are written on and you may have to go through the whole process again if you lose your Deed Poll because it isn't registered officially. The UK Deed Poll Service is probably your safest bet because it is the government-authorised body, which means it archives your records and allows you to order copies. You also get a certificate printed on watermarked paper to indicate it is bona fide.

DID YOU KNOW...? NO SEX OR FAKE TITLES

Although in principle you can change your name to anything you like – Jane and Thomas Love's Young Dream, for instance – in practice the officials in charge of Deed Polls frown on anything that could be used fraudulently. So you can't trade up and become Lord Thomas Green and Lady Jane Green just by applying. Similarly, anything they consider vulgar, blasphemous or downright unsuitable will be rejected. The rule is at least one forename and one surname, and no numbers or symbols.

AT A GLANCE WEDDING PLANNER

With so many big plans and small details to consider it is easy to forget something on your list. The following wedding planner gives a round up of key elements you may be including in your big day, and gives an idea of when they should be organised.

How it works

For the purposes of the table we've assumed a wedding planned one year ahead. If your wedding is being organised in a shorter or longer timeframe you can still use the planner, just adjust it to suit your own schedule.

You may find it helpful to photocopy the planner and keep it in your diary, or pinned to the kitchen wall.

Simply use the tick boxes to indicate when something has been sorted out and add additional notes such as dates, contacts or phone numbers next to each item on your list. Remember to keep supporting paperwork such as contracts together in a box file or folder.

12 Months +

☐ Set date for wedding . . . .

☐ Decide on wedding style . . . .

☐ Set budget . . . .

☐ Arrange wedding finance (if necessary) . . . .

☐ Book church/register office/wedding venue . . . .

☐ Book reception venue/organise marquee . . . .

☐ Shortlist and select caterers . . . .

☐ Plan engagement party/parties . . . .

9 Months +

☐ Review budget . . . .

☐ Decide on best man/attendants . . . .

☐ Draw up guest list . . . .

☐ Start thinking about wedding outfits . . . .

☐ Start planning honeymoon . . . .

☐ Book time off work for honeymoon . . . .

☐ Start planning stag/hen parties . . . .

6 Months +

- [ ] Tie up legalities for wedding (e.g. banns) ....
- [ ] Decide on/book reception entertainment ....
- [ ] Go shopping for wedding outfits ....
- [ ] Select florist ....
- [ ] Book cake maker ....
- [ ] Book honeymoon ....
- [ ] Organise wedding transport ....
- [ ] Select photographer/videographer ....

3 Months +

- [ ] Review budget ....
- [ ] Finalise details of wedding service (e.g. music, readings) ....
- [ ] Send out invitations ....
- [ ] Review/finalise menu ....
- [ ] Organise bar/drinks ....
- [ ] Check deposits for venue, etc. are paid ....
- [ ] Ensure passports are up to date ....
- [ ] Finalise wedding outfits ....
- [ ] Agree final budget on flowers ....
- [ ] Book pre-wedding hair/beauty appointments ....
- [ ] Order/buy gifts for helpers (parents, best man, bridesmaids, etc.) ....

1 Month +

- [ ] Draw up/print order of service (if religious ceremony) ....
- [ ] Organise wedding rehearsal (for church weddings) ....
- [ ] Final fittings for wedding outfits ....
- [ ] Chase wedding replies ....
- [ ] Confirm final numbers with reception venue ....
- [ ] Check honeymoon travel paperwork ....
- [ ] Reconfirm/check wedding transport ....

1 Week +

- [ ] Go over any last-minute checks with reception venue ....
- [ ] Try on wedding outfits with all accessories ....
- [ ] Reconfirm timings with best man, bridesmaids and ushers ....
- [ ] Relax – and get some beauty sleep ....

TROUBLESHOOTING

✧ MANAGING AN OVERSPEND

'My girlfriend is going mad with all the details (helped by her mother) and I'm afraid we are going to blow our budget completely.'

It's easily done, and who can blame her for wanting to make the wedding day special? But you have to intervene with a 'reality check' before it goes too far.

1 No one wants to appear mean, but it makes no sense at all to host a wedding you can't afford and you need to sit down with your girlfriend and go through the money spent so far and the commitments she is about to make. Avoid accusing her of over-spending – it is better to say something along the lines of 'I'm worried about this because I don't think we can afford it.'

2 Avoid raising the topic with her in front of her mother – this may just cause tension – and don't feel you have to continually justify your unwillingness to spend more than you can afford.

3 Try and get some sort of accounting system going if you haven't done so up to now. This can be a simple book, but writing down the money spent will make her think twice and could inspire her to make savings herself. See if there is anything you can shave off the budget spent so far. If she hasn't finalised payment for everything there may be economies you can make.

4 Get more involved yourself. You can't blame her if you didn't keep an eye on the finances too. Perhaps sit down once a fortnight just to see where you are, and also ask if you can take over some of the organising.

✧ NAME CHANGE DILEMMA

'When I told my future in-laws I intended to keep my maiden name they reacted really strangely. Now I'm afraid it is going to cause problems between us.'

The older generation can struggle with modern conventions and this appears to be the case with your in-laws. You need to understand why they are upset, and also explain your case.

1 You can't skirt round this issue so it is best to talk to your in-laws directly to find out why they don't approve. They may feel offended that their name isn't 'good enough' or have some wild idea that you are intending to have an open marriage with their son. Whatever is concerning them, find out.

2 Have some justifications ready for why you are keeping your maiden name. It could be that you don't agree with the tradition on equality grounds, or that you feel you need to keep your identity. Perhaps you have good professional reasons for continuing to use your maiden name. While you may not think this is a big issue, they do, so try to give them the most logical explanation you can.

3 Reassure them that you will be truly married to their son and are proud to be a member of their family – a small but important statement that may overcome their fears about your decision.

4 Don't be too adamant about keeping your maiden name in every situation. While officially your name isn't changing it is not necessary to inform everyone at the wedding that you are still a Ms. And it doesn't hurt your equal status and shouldn't hurt your feelings if some older relatives or friends start calling you by your husband's name. See it for what it is – a detail.

CHAPTER 5

THE BIG DAY

For many couples the wedding celebration passes in a flash. After weeks or months of preparation you can finally relax, let your hair down and enjoy the party. This is not the time to panic over last-minute preparations, but you do want the formalities to run like clockwork. This chapter outlines timings and seating plans for the wedding ceremony plus tips on ensuring the reception runs smoothly. There's advice on the speeches, first dance and final goodbyes to your guests – even a few pointers on getting die-hard party animals to pack up and go home.

GET ME TO THE CHURCH ON TIME

Whether it's a religious ceremony, register office or wedding venue, your key priority on the wedding morning is to get there promptly and in as unflustered a state as possible. Here are points to remember.

✧ TRANSPORT

Whether you have booked a wedding car or enlisted a friend as driver, you need to ensure the route to the ceremony has been properly timed in advance of the wedding day. If you are unsure of the length of the journey, or the best route to your wedding venue, do a practice run the week before, remembering to travel on the same day at around the same time. Also bear in mind one-off events, such as roadworks, sporting fixtures or the town carnival, which might make the traffic heavier than usual. Everyone in the wedding party, bar the bridal party and bridesmaids/bride's mother, should aim to be at the wedding venue at least 20 minutes before the ceremony is scheduled to start. Do check this with your minister/registrar in case they need you there earlier than that.

✧ TIMINGS AND TRAVEL COMPANIONS

- Ushers make their way to the wedding using their own transport. It is crucial that they arrive early – at least 40 minutes before the service is scheduled to start.
- Bridegroom's father and mother travel together – arriving 30 minutes early so they can help greet early-bird guests.
- The groom and best man should be the first of the wedding party to arrive. Normally they travel to the venue together.
- Bridesmaids and the bride's mother travel together. They arrive shortly before the bride and wait for her outside the wedding venue. The bride's mother is traditionally the last guest to be seated.
- The bride and her father (or the person giving her away) traditionally arrive together in one car. If no one is giving the bride away she may choose to travel with her chief bridesmaid or mother.

LAST-MINUTE CHECKLIST

Rings Don't forget the two key essentials. The bride's ring should be with her father or the person who will hand it to her during the service. The best man should guard the groom's ring.

Travel documents If you're heading straight off on honeymoon you will need your travel tickets and passport. Have these taken in advance to the reception venue and stored in your room or the hotel safe. You will also need your honeymoon luggage packed and ready.

Flowers Don't forget buttonholes, bouquets and any other floral accessories you will be wearing to the church or register office.

Change of clothes If you are changing for the evening party or donning a going away outfit this should be entrusted to the best man, chief bridesmaid or someone who can get it to your venue for you in an uncrushed condition.

Cards and Telemessages Any post that will be read out at the reception needs to be gathered together and delivered to the reception venue for the best man to announce in his speech. If you have time,

sort through it first to decide which cards and messages take priority.

Make up For the bride it's useful to have a small bag of kit for emergency touch-ups. Essentials might include spare tights/ stockings, hair-grips, hairspray, tissues, lipstick, powder and make up remover pads/cotton buds (in case you cry). Entrust this to the bride's mother or chief bridesmaid.

First aid Get someone to carry emergency supplies of headache pills, anti-histamine (for hay fever attacks/insect stings) and antacid tablets. Useful for the happy couple or anyone else in the wedding party.

Bottled water Ensure both the bride and groom's cars have water in them. A dry mouth is a standard pre-wedding nervous symptom. Water will help.

Cash Like the Queen, the happy couple can hand over cash to someone else for the day. Usually the best man keeps a stash of notes on him. You might also want to ensure the bride and groom's fathers have their wallets primed and ready.

✧ DON'T KEEP THEM WAITING

Although by tradition the bride kept the groom waiting, many wedding venues take a dim view of tardiness and if you are very late they may refuse to marry you altogether. You will find that most register offices ask you to turn up at least 10 minutes before the service so they can finalise the legal paperwork, and if it's a religious ceremony the official holding it is likely to give you a fixed arrival time. Obviously delays can happen on the day (have a mobile phone with you just in case the car breaks down or you get stuck in traffic), but being late because you can amounts to rudeness if there are other weddings following yours. Also bear in mind that you have a crowd of guests waiting for you; a delay can be frustrating for them, especially if there are young children who need to be kept occupied.

✧ WHO SITS WHERE?

In churches, normally the bride's party are seated on the left and the bridegroom's on the right. Avoid 'back of the bus' mentality by getting ushers to lead guests to their seats – filling up the wedding venue from the front (behind pews reserved for the wedding party) to allow space for latecomers to slip in and find a seat near the back. This also makes the wedding venue seem fuller – useful if yours is a small ceremony. If one family has far more guests than the other you may decide to abandon tradition and split guests equally on either side of the church.

In register offices there can be a variety of seating configurations – check this before the day, but you may find it easier to abandon traditional his and hers seating plans and let people sit where they like. Remember that seats should be reserved for the bridal party and family; normally this would include immediate family, close relatives and key helpers such as the mothers of young bridesmaids/pages.

✧ ORDER OF SERVICE

This is not an essential, but at church weddings it is a nice touch to include a printed sheet detailing the nature of the service, hymns and prayers, plus additional information about music played or special readings. For many older guests this is a souvenir of the day that they will want to keep. It is fine to design and print these out for yourself – indeed it makes them more personal – although you can get them prepared by a professional printer, provided the details of the service are finalised in good time. Ushers hand the sheets/booklets out to guests when they arrive or ensure they are placed on seats or pew ends.

DID YOU KNOW...? WHY THE DOORS STAY UNLOCKED

Officially a wedding is a public ceremony and that means that doors to the room where the ceremony is being held must be left unlocked. This is a legal obligation – and gives anyone the chance to enter and either witness the marriage taking place or make their objection before it does. Fortunately, few people think it is a good idea to crash other people's weddings and objections to the marriage taking place are even rarer.

THE SERVICE
✧ CHURCH OF ENGLAND AND WALES

The minister will talk you through the order of service before the wedding, giving you a chance to choose certain elements. There may also be a rehearsal so you can run through timings and learn where to stand during the wedding. The service is normally a short introduction by the minister welcoming the congregation and explaining Christian belief in marriage. After that he or she will ask if anyone knows any reasons why the couple may not be married. With that hurdle crossed, the ceremony itself takes place with first the groom and then the bride repeating the marriage vows and swapping rings. After that the minister declares you husband and wife and then says prayers and/or a blessing. A short service of readings and a sermon generally follows before the signing of the register.

✧ REGISTER OFFICE OR CIVIL VENUE?

The registrar will normally agree the details of the service in advance, including any music or poetry readings. You will also fill in a short form detailing the wording you want for the service (there are usually three options) and can decide how you make your entrance. The bride can enter after the groom or the couple can enter the room together before or after their guests. The ceremony itself normally lasts around 15–20 minutes and after a short welcome by the superintendent registrar, during which an explanation is given of the civil marriage service, the bride and groom repeat their vows and exchange rings. After that the second registrar completes the marriage certificate and this is signed by the couple and their two witnesses.

✧ OTHER RELIGIOUS SERVICES

Most services follow a broadly similar process of vow making in order to solemnise a marriage, but there are many differences in the length of service and the wording used. For more information you need to contact the minister marrying you who will run through the outline of the service and explain the options open to you. Additional information is also available via websites. See the Religious ceremonies section of Useful Sources (page 120).

DID YOU KNOW...? CHANGING SIDES

In church weddings if the bride is being given away she enters the church holding her father's right arm and stands on the left of the groom. Once she has been married she takes her husband's left arm to walk back down the aisle on the other side of the church. If the bride is not being given away she can enter the church alone, or with her future husband if she prefers.

RECORDING YOUR WEDDING

Photos and videos capture your big day forever, but the temptation can be to let them take over and hold up proceedings. Before you start committing to print/video remember a few rules.

- First and foremost, get permission from the church/register office/wedding venue if you plan to take cameras or video cameras into their premises. Some are willing, many are not.

You may also have to pay them a copyright fee if video recording takes place.

- If you choose professionals, ensure not only that their work is up to standard but also their professional manner meets your approval. None of your guests will enjoy being bullied or having a camera capturing them with their mouth full.
- Don't get carried away. It isn't necessary to record every last second. And you will find it hard to concentrate on enjoying yourself while the cameras are on you.
- Be strict with guests who are keen amateur photographers or videographers – they shouldn't be allowed to get in the way of the professionals or hold up proceedings.

✧ THE PHOTOGRAPHS

Everyone has been to weddings where the photos take an age and it can be a problem if you have either an over-enthusiastic photographer or a large crowd to be photographed. Here's how to plan the shoot so it doesn't cut into valuable party time.

- Talk to your photographer in advance to outline exactly how many shots you want. Also check how photography is charged – by time or by shot.
- Decide on the sort of shots you want – traditional formal poses are giving way to more naturalistic portraits. A compromise might be to choose a mixture of the two.
- Resist all entreaties if you don't want to be snapped kissing behind a brandy glass or embracing under a lych gate. These are your mementos not your photographer's.
- Plan with your photographer in advance where the photos should be taken. Outdoor shots are generally both flattering and easier to set up, but have a contingency plan in case the weather is grey and rainy.
- Bear in mind that you may pay more if you ask your photographer to move on to your reception venue. But if shots are restricted to church/register office the wedding following yours could cut down your time.

- It is normal to include group shots to mark the attendance of your guests, but get someone (ideally the best man) to round up the people who need to be photographed together. They will need to mix tact with drill sergeant tactics.
- Don't rely on your photographer alone. One trick is to issue guests with disposable cameras, either individually or one per table. Another easy way to supplement the formal poses is to ask friends to get extra copies of their best prints so you can add to your album.

FORMAL PHOTOS

There are tried and trusted routines for the group shots at a wedding. Normally these would be bride and groom with the following:

Both sets of parents

Parents plus best man and bridesmaids

Best man and bridesmaids

Groom's immediate family

Bride's immediate family

Ushers

Group shots of guests – split into bride/groom's side or male/female if it's a large wedding

✦ THE VIDEO

While it used to be the craze to record every last party moment, these days some couples prefer to do without the live highlights of their wedding. If you choose to have your wedding filmed remember the following.

- Check the rates of a professional carefully. You should expect to pay from £500 plus, but ask what this includes. Also check what equipment they will be using – modern cameras are smaller and less intrusive.
- Ask to see examples of their work – and find out if they are members of a professional association (e.g. Association of Professional Videomakers).

- Check how the video will be delivered. For instance, will they edit it before you see it? Do they set it to a soundtrack? If so, who chooses the soundtrack?
- Don't let them take over. Gone are the days of trailing wires and huge lights but filming can still be intrusive and there may be moments that you don't want on camera. Also, no one (not even you) wants to sit through an epic – filming should capture the best moments, not relive the whole day.
- One way to cut costs is to go with an amateur recording. Just ensure the person behind the camera knows what they are doing and isn't too closely involved with the wedding itself (i.e. not the bride's father or the best man).

True life stories: Our friends took the photos
Marilyn and Leo knew they wanted a more informal style wedding and that included the wedding photos. 'My mum wanted lots of posed shots but I just didn't like the idea and I knew I'd never want to display the end results,' says Marilyn. They decided to let their friends record the day – some came armed with their own cameras and tables at the reception were issued with disposable cameras, which were collected at the end of the evening. 'We had hundreds of shots to look through and although some were definitely not for the album others really summed up the day. There were even a few good portraits of us in there. We love them because they have a more relaxed feel, and having friends' viewpoints of the day seems more personal somehow.'

RECEPTION PRACTICALITIES

The party begins in earnest once you and your guests get to the reception, but for bride and groom there are a few more hurdles to cross. Here's how to manage the formalities.

✧ RECEPTION LINE

This is not an essential at the wedding, but it is one sure way to ensure you speak to all your guests at least once – even if it is only to greet them and thank them for coming.

- Normally, the reception line includes the bride's mother and father, groom's mother and father and the bride and groom (standing in that order).
- If either side's parents are divorced you need to discuss details with them and come up with a workable compromise. It could be mother and father only or both parents plus new partners – just bear in mind that the line will take longer than usual.
- One modern alternative is to leave parents out altogether and have the bride and groom do the greeting alone. Or you could avoid the reception line and walk around the tables as a couple to say your hellos.
- Decide in advance where the reception line should stand, avoiding narrow entrances or dimly lit corridors if you can. Also spare a thought for less able guests – they should be assisted to the front of the queue so they don't have to stand for too long.
- Your guests will find it easier to wait if they have been handed a welcome drink first.
- Be prepared to speed things up if there's a bottleneck. A discreet coded nod or wink to parents should ensure that whoever is being over talkative gets side-tracked into a conversation by the next in line and the queue gets moving again.

WHAT TO DO WITH PRESENTS?

Although you may have a gift list, it's almost inevitable that some guests will turn up armed with presents. Thank them profusely, but resist the temptation to open the gifts – not only will this stop you talking to your other guests, but you will also be more likely to break the gift or lose the accompanying gift tag, making it impossible to write and thank them later. Instead, set up a secured area well away from the throng of guests and get an usher or bridesmaid to store gifts there. Get them to ask the guest if there's a label with the gift, and if there isn't ensure they write one there and then so it can be identified later (issue your helper with plain labels, pens and some sticky tape). Put your best man in charge of organising the safe transport of gifts to your parents' home after the party.

✧ SEATING PLAN

Whether it's a formal top-table affair or a relaxed buffet, your guests will be looking to you for advice on where to go and what to do next. This is where the ushers and best man can be invaluable – get them to marshal the crowds by showing them where the table plans are or letting them know it's a sit anywhere affair. If the plan is detailed, site it so that people can see it without a crush (or set up two at opposite ends of the room).

Formal seating plan

At traditional weddings there's a 'top table', usually placed at right angles to the guests' tables so everyone can see the guests of honour and hear their speeches. There are two standard variations on the plan:

TOP TABLE VARIATION 1							
best man	chief bridesmaid	groom's father	bride's mother	bridegroom	bride	bride's father	groom's mother

TOP TABLE VARIATION 2							
groom's mother	groom's father	bride's mother	groom	bride	bride's father	best man	chief bridesmaid

The tables nearest the top table are reserved for bride's family and groom's family. There are many variations on the plans shown above, but your main aim is to ensure everyone on the top table is comfortable with their position and that you sit in the centre next to each other. If following convention is going to put a dampener on proceedings – for instance, if divorced parents really don't get on – then set your own rules. You could have a top table consisting of the wedding party (best man, chief bridesmaid, etc.) and get parents to act as hosts on other tables, with their new partners.

Consider round tables

If space won't allow a long top table, or you prefer a less formal approach, you can sit at a round table, with guests arranged around you. The advantage is that more people have close access to the top table and you don't feel like you are on show all the time. The disadvantage is that some guests will have a view of your back. With round tables, the bride and groom can sit together and arrange key guests around them (see Top Table diagrams), or they can sit facing each other. Your wedding venue or marquee hire company may be able to suggest other configurations, depending on the size of the venue and the number of guests you are entertaining.

Where to seat your guests

In the old days there was a strict hierarchy – 'also inviteds' knew their place, and it was usually a long way from the bride and groom. These days, people are a lot more inclusive at weddings and, as no one wants to feel as though they are in the duff seat, it is worth revising your plan until it feels as if everyone will be in congenial company. Here are some pointers.

- Once you have decided your table configurations, cut out pieces of card with the names of guests and then stick them on the diagram. This allows you to juggle names around until you find a layout that feels right.
- Do place couples together – no one wants to sit miles away from their partner, particularly if they know no one else at the wedding.
- Put like with like – elderly aunties and uncles will love the chance to catch up with each other so place them together. Similarly, nieces and nephews/old school friends have plenty of shared ground so that will ensure a lively table.
- Give families with young children plenty of space and easy access to the bathrooms/garden. That way they can slip in and out without disturbing other guests if the kids get restless. Putting family groups close together ensures the parents get to chat to people in a similar situation without feeling obliged to apologise about upset drinks or food fights.

- Be wary of placing divorced couples/exes close together. Ideally put them on different tables at different ends of the room. Parents should be the exception – it's their job to be civil for the day.
- Be sensitive with singles. They don't want to be isolated on a table full of couples. Nor do they want to be obviously shoehorned next to someone you think is a match made in heaven. Ideally, get all your single friends together on the same table/s.
- Abandon the boy/girl configuration if it isn't going to work. Sometimes it is the one irritating detail that gets in the way of your perfect seating plan.

DON'T FORGET TO EAT SOMETHING

Many brides and grooms get through their wedding day with barely a drop to eat or drink, but it's vital that you eat something at the reception or you won't make it to the end of the day. Tucking in can also be intimidating since so many people are watching you; and you don't want to spill tomato coulis all over your wedding finery. If you can't stomach the full meal then eat the starter, pick at the main course and fill up on bread rolls. A few forkfuls of dessert or wedding cake will also help by raising your blood sugar level. Remember to mix alcohol with non-alcoholic drinks so you can stay hydrated (particularly important on a hot summer's day). Order bottled water for the top table – tonic water or lemonade in a tall glass full of ice if you don't want your guests to think you are avoiding the merrymaking.

MANAGING SMALL CHILDREN

A roomful of guests can normally absorb a few tiny tearaways but if you have lots of young children it can be a good idea to lay on extra entertainment for them. Some couples organise childminders, a bouncy castle or children's entertainers. Before you book anyone do check their credentials, their insurance and their expectations. For instance, it is no good scheduling a children's entertainer during the meal if they expect parents to be in attendance to watch their children. Also ensure you get an exact number of children if you're laying on childminding – even one too many may invalidate their insurance cover.

SPEECHES, TOASTS AND CAKE CUTTING

These are the final formalities before bride and groom get to relax and enjoy the party. You can make as much or as little of them as you like. Here are the traditional conventions:

✧ THE SPEAKERS

Normally the speeches begin after the meal has ended – after or during coffee/desert is typical. They run in the following order and include the following bare essentials.

- **Bride's father** Thanks guests for coming and says a few words about his daughter and son-in-law. Toasts the bride and groom.
- **Bridegroom** Says how thrilled and lucky he is, thanks parents/in-laws and any other important contributors (e.g. dressmaker/florist) before toasting the beautiful bridesmaids.
- **Best man** Thanks bride's father and groom for their speeches and traditionally (though this is not always observed) replies on behalf of the bridesmaids by thanking the groom for his toast. Reads out Telemessages/cards from people who can't be there. Pokes fun at bridegroom and includes one or two pithy anecdotes before toasting the happy couple.

  The best man should also act as ringmaster, introducing each of the speakers. Ensure he keeps a mental note of who has been thanked just in case an essential person has been left off – it's fine for him to add another thank you at the end.

✧ ADDITIONAL SPEAKERS

You don't have to observe the convention on speaking – many brides decide it is too one-sided. The bride, chief bridesmaid, bride's mother or any other representative the bride or groom choose can also make a speech. One word of caution though, if everyone has their five-minutes' worth, you risk losing your audience to drink or drowsiness. The solution is to be strict on timings – allowing everyone just two or three minutes. Also, get a bit of information about the speeches to ensure there won't be too much repetition or too many nostalgic stories.

TALK FIRST

A variation finding increasing favour is to have speeches before everyone eats. The benefits are twofold: the best man and other speech givers get to enjoy their meal and no one has to worry about not drinking. On the downside, speeches traditionally act as a punctuation mark between the formality of dining and the more relaxed dancing and mingling phases of the wedding. If you do decide to speak before the meal it is a good idea to use the cake-cutting ceremony to mark the end of 'formalities'.

UNACCUSTOMED AS I AM...

Here are six essential tips for novice and experienced speakers, to ensure the speeches flow smoothly and your audience enjoy the occasion:

1 **Keep it short and simple** It is better to speak fluently for three minutes than stumble on hopelessly for six. Time your speech, use simple ideas and words and introduce clear punctuation points (e.g. thanks, jokes and toasts) so guests know where you are going and when you are going to get there!

2 **Use notes** Experienced speakers know how easy it is to dry up so have some key words or phrases written onto small cards. Even if you don't use them, you will feel more confident. This also gives you something to do with your hands – useful if you have a tendency to wave them about while you're speaking.

3 **Practise first** Rehearse in front of a mirror, a friend, or even the dog. Get used to saying the words out loud so you can time yourself and work out if a clever joke or piece of wordplay is going to be too difficult to pull off on the day.

4 **Slow down** Timing is everything so don't swallow your best lines or gallop through the all-important thank-yous. Introduce pauses and remember to listen to your audience and break for laughter and applause.

5 **Keep it clean** Everyone expects jokes, but you should never stray too far from convention. If in doubt, imagine what the oldest and staidest person in the room is likely to think of the sentiment/language.

6 **Relax** Enjoy the moment because this is the kindest audience you will ever get. They are willing you to do well and be funny, and it won't take much to bring the house down.

✧ THE CAKE CUTTING

Once the speeches are finished the cake-cutting ceremony takes place. This is the final official photocall event for the bride and groom and many guests will want to get their cameras at the ready, so it is a good idea to announce it a few minutes in advance. Once the cake is cut it is generally removed so it can be sliced properly and offered to guests either with their coffee or later during the party.

Position the cake so everyone can see it and photograph you, and ensure you are armed with a decent knife – it would be a terrible shame to destroy your carefully iced creation. Also remember that this is a ceremonial cut rather than a divvying up process. The bridegroom places his hands over the bride's and then they push the knife down very gently (no karate chops), smile sweetly for the audience and hand the rest of the cutting over to the pros.

DID YOU KNOW...? DIVIDING UP THE CAKE

Traditionally, a tier of the wedding cake was reserved for the first child's christening. If it is an iced fruitcake there should be no problem storing it in an airtight tin for several years, but tell your cake maker if you would like to observe this convention. Another old tradition was to send pieces of cake to guests who couldn't attend the wedding. This is not observed so often these days but you can buy small boxes for posting slices to absent friends.

PARTY TIME

With the final reception formalities out of the way you can relax and enjoy the party. This is your chance to mingle with your family, catch up with friends you haven't seen in ages and take to the dance floor as a married couple.

✧ FIRST DANCE

If you have live music or a DJ then everyone will expect the happy couple to take to the dance floor first. Until you do this then the party won't really get going. For some people this is a trial, but even if you're a 'can't dance, won't dance' type of girl or guy, it simply has to be done. Here are tips for the shy and/or left footed:

- **Pick the music** Everyone has something they love to dance to. So prime the DJ or band to start this song when you are ready to take to the floor and then you can dance without worrying about missing a beat. Make sure they play the right version, not a DJ remix or a souped-up remake of a slow number.
- **Practise first** Not essential, but if you think you simply can't cut it on the night without trying out a few dance moves, do this in the privacy of your own bedroom. And if you want to wow them with your ballroom moves, you can even take a few lessons (see Trip the light fantastic, page 105).
- **Loosen your tie/tiara** It can be hard enough to dance in front of a crowd, almost impossible if you are constricted by your wedding finery. It is fine at this point in the evening to let your hair down and remove wedding veil, jacket, tie or shoes if that makes you feel more comfortable.
- **Press gang some friends** If you are really uncomfortable about the spotlight being on you, speak to your best man, chief bridesmaid and any other willing guests. All you have to do as a couple is sashay onto the dance floor, take a couple of quick steps and then they join you. This is also the very best way to get the rest of the guests onto the dance floor.

SIX FAVOURITE FIRST DANCE TRACKS

Here are six popular tracks to start off the dancing:

Can't help falling in love, ELVIS PRESLEY

Angels, ROBBIE WILLIAMS

Nobody does it better, CARLY SIMON

When a man loves a woman, PERCY SLEDGE

You're the best thing, STYLE COUNCIL

Stand by me, BEN E KING

✧ HOW TO GET THEM DANCING

We've all been to weddings where one super-slow or totally obscure track cleared the dance floor in under a minute. Fine if it's time for everyone to go home, but pacing and selecting music is a fine art and you should never leave choices up to the DJ alone. Tell them you need something to appeal to every age group at the party so it's fine to stick Sinatra or Crosby alongside anthems that appeal to the twenty-somethings. Avoid B-sides, unknown album tracks and long party remixes unless they are particular favourites of yours. If in doubt about the mix, just add in more classics from the '70s and '80s since these are familiar enough to have really broad appeal. The first hour and last 20 minutes should be the liveliest, but pace things by including slower tracks in between.

✧ WHEN IT'S TIME TO GO HOME...

And for when the party's over, here are a few subtle tricks to help tell guests it's time to go home.

- **Have a going away ceremony** Even if you are just retreating to your room for a well-earned glass of champagne or foot massage, this is a useful way of indicating to guests that the party is just about over. Throw your bouquet, hug and kiss your family and wave a tearful or joyful goodbye to your guests.
- **Get the DJ to call time** The best way to do this is to ask everyone up onto the dance floor for a final hurrah because the music will

stop in 10 minutes. In reality there are still 20 minutes to go, but this ensures everyone will end the evening on a high note as well as being so worn out they feel ready to adjourn to their beds.

- **Change the music** The last and most underhand option is to switch from disco to sleep-inducing romantic tracks. While a few barflies will be left staring moodily into their drinks, most people will feel a sudden urge to grab their coats and go.

✧ ...AND WHAT NOT TO DO

These are the things you should avoid at all costs – unless you want people to remember your party as a washout.

- **Switch on the lights** As atmosphere killers go this is the big one. Suddenly that dim-lit room full of glamorous people is revealed as a hot and dishevelled throng of drunks.
- **Start clearing up** Any hint of a vacuum cleaner or busy person armed with spray cleaner is downright rude. If you are at a venue, make it quite clear that they don't start clearing tables overtly until the guests have departed.
- **Disappear and leave them to it** You're entitled to depart but someone from the wedding party needs to be at their post until the bitter end. The most suitable person is the best man, since he can also ensure taxis are called and do final checks to make sure there's no one sleeping in the shrubbery.

DID YOU KNOW...? IT'S 'RUDE' TO LEAVE BEFORE THE BRIDE

If you don't plan a going away ceremony – perhaps because you intend to wring the most out of every last moment – then let your older relatives and friends know what is happening in advance of the evening. They come from a generation that thought it wasn't appropriate to leave before the bride and groom had departed, which could be a struggle for them if you're still hogging the dancefloor at 2am.

TROUBLESHOOTING

✧ WORRIED ABOUT TIMINGS

'I'm terrified my wedding is going to go off track because of the length of the reception line and the number of guests to be greeted. Also, my mother wants photographs taken before we get to sit down and eat.'

Talkative parents or an extended photocall can hijack your plans to seat and feed your guests. You need to do some military-style planning, and make a few compromises.

1 Review your schedules and be realistic about the extra time that you are going to take to get your guests seated. It is better to tell the caterers in advance so they can plan accordingly. If you build in an extra half-hour before the meal begins this will take the stress off you. Do ensure, however, that the photographer knows the deadline and that the others in the reception line keep an eye on their watches.

2 Consider if you can shift the photographer's timings a little. For instance, is it possible to have some photos taken before you leave your home for the wedding ceremony? Because you have a fixed deadline this will encourage him or her to work efficiently and your mother to accept that there are limitations on the number of shots.

3 Restrict the reception line to you and your spouse. This is the most drastic option, but many couples choose not to organise a long meet and greet because it cuts into the party. Alternatives include getting your guests seated and then going to greet them. Or you and your partner could simply make a short welcome speech before you all tuck into your meal.

✧ DREADING HIS SPEECH

'My girlfriend's father is a great raconteur and I'm sure his speech is going to last forever. Is there anything I can do to encourage him to keep it short?'

You may be almost family, but you're not there yet so this is not something to raise with him yourself. Diplomacy is not, however, essential from your future mother-in-law or wife. Here are some options.

1 Talk to your fiancée first and just mention that you are worried about the length of the speeches. If she is wise to her father's rambling tendencies then she might be as anxious about it as you. Rather than approach him and ask him to shorten his speech, a better move on her part might be to tell him all speakers are restricting themselves to five minutes.

2 Approach your future mother-in-law and ask if she knows roughly how long her husband's speech will last. Do this under the guise that you are confirming final details with the caterers. If she thinks his speech is going to upset all the timings she may encourage him – in her own unique way – to keep it brief.

3 Do nothing. This may sound the cowardly option but on balance does it really matter if he goes on a bit? This is his big day too and surely your guests will forgive a slightly longer than normal speech from a proud and beaming father of the bride?

✧ KEEPING A RAVER IN CHECK

'My uncle enjoys a drink but it tends to relax all his inhibitions; at my cousin's wedding he was an embarrassment. How can I keep him from ruining my wedding?'

With only one relative to worry about, a lot of couples would call you lucky! While you may think he is going to let the side down most of your guests will forgive his 'eccentricity'. Here's an action plan that may help keep him in check and allow you to relax.

1 Nominate a few large men – say, best man, brother and an usher – to be his minders. They can shadow him discreetly and monitor his drinking levels. One of the best methods of cutting down on his drinking is to engage him in conversation, get him onto the dance floor or take him off to admire someone's marvellous new car (no test driving though).

2 If his minders think he is getting unruly they can offer to go to the bar for him and then start replacing alcoholic with non-alcoholic drinks. Or get them to doctor the drinks – spirits can be served in quarter measures, wine mixed with water, or beer delivered in half pint glasses. They should also take a long time to get back from the bar with each drink.

3 Should things get really out of hand (e.g. drunken striptease) then get the minders to quietly but firmly remove him from public view. He may curse them at the time but he'll be grateful when it comes to the next morning. Tell them to avoid reasoning with him in front of your guests; it's unlikely to work and may cause more of a scene.

4 Having done your best to manage the situation from afar, relax and accept that you can't be responsible for his behaviour. Your guests will be more understanding than you give them credit for – after all, they have families too.

CHAPTER 6

THE HONEYMOON & AFTER

After the wedding is the honeymoon, and by the time their wedding day arrives, many couples are holding out for the holiday. In this chapter are tips for planning the perfect romantic break – including working out where to go – and advice to ensure you tie up all the loose ends from your wedding when you finally arrive back home.

THE HONEYMOON

This is supposed to be a magical trip, so who can blame you for worrying about the details and wanting to get it just right? Here are some pointers:

✧ WHO DECIDES ON THE DESTINATION?

In the old days, the honeymoon was invariably the 'surprise, surprise' element of the wedding. It was chosen by the groom and many brides had no idea where they were going, or for how long. But these days many couples decide that this is a joint decision and something they should both plan and pay for. Here are pros and cons.

Surprise

Pros:

• Married life starts as an adventure – and surprises are always exciting.
• For the bride there is one less thing to plan or worry about.

Cons:

• All the weight falls on the groom – so if the resort doesn't live up to expectations or it rains every day then he feels responsible.
• The bride may spend hours worrying about what to pack or take her entire wardrobe along in order to cope with every eventuality.

Pre-arranged destination

Pros:

• Both parties get something to look forward to; anticipation is often half the fun of a holiday.
• There's time to plan side trips or adventures so the holiday is geared perfectly towards both sides' tastes.

Cons:

• You may spend hours trying to work out where to go and what to do – especially if this is an extended trip or you like different holiday experiences.

- Joint planning takes time and may add an extra level of stress to your wedding preparations.

True life stories: Travelling light

Keeping your wife-to-be in the dark about the honeymoon destination only works if you are prepared to brief her properly. For Nicole, it was a surprise that could have gone horribly wrong. 'My husband's idea of the perfect holiday wardrobe is a bit different to mine so every time I asked what I should pack he just said "shorts",' says Nicole. 'The closer we got to the wedding the more nervous I became. Finally, a week before we were due to go, I decided I couldn't bear the suspense and begged him to tell me. It turned out to be a cruise round the Caribbean, so if I had just packed cut-offs and a swimsuit I would have felt pretty uncomfortable dining at the captain's table.'

✧ AND WHO PAYS?

The honeymoon can turn into a major wedding expense, so it's important to decide on both the budget and the way you will share the cost.

Traditionally, paying for the honeymoon was down to the bridegroom, but since this tradition dates back to the days when the bride's side had stumped up for the wedding you may want to take a fairer approach. The other factor to consider is cost – a week in a boarding house in Bridlington might have been within the reach of most grooms, three weeks in South America is another thing altogether.

✧ MAKING IT SPECIAL

The pressure can be on to organise 'the holiday of a lifetime', but this isn't necessary if you have blown your budget on a fabulous wedding or have commitments to a mortgage or job. There will be other holidays (plus second and third honeymoons) so focus on what you want and can afford. It doesn't have to be a long trip either – a weekend in a world class hotel will probably furnish you with more memories than two weeks at a standard beach resort. Here are things to remember before you book:

- **Book with the season** If sunshine is vital to you, then chase the good weather not the destination. In particular you might want to steer clear of hurricane season in the Caribbean and monsoons in Asia. It's information that your travel agent should tell you, so if something looks a bargain then ask about the likely rainfall or any other seasonal problems you might encounter.
- **Remember spending money** Don't stretch your budget so far that you end up in the world's most glamorous location with barely enough cash left to order a Mai Tai. It will feel far more special to choose a more modest resort and have extra money so you can enjoy blow-out meals, boat trips and cocktails at sunset.
- **Don't be shoehorned** If you're not beach people or you hate the idea of being surrounded by other honeymooners then avoid the packages that promise romance. You can make your own special moments doing what it is you love – be it climbing, caravanning or simply mooching about in cafés.
- **Build in something memorable** Even the most budget-strapped honeymooners should reserve spare cash to make this a momentous holiday. It could be a meal in a five-star restaurant, a session at the casino or learning to water ski/scuba dive. This is the sure-fire way to create unforgettable memories.

CHECK YOUR TRAVEL INSURANCE

For any holiday you need travel insurance, but this is one occasion when it is worth taking out extra cover just in case you decide to try sports that are classified as dangerous. Check with your insurer what the exclusion clauses are and then consider upgrading if you think you might want to live a little more dangerously than usual.

True life stories: A DIY honeymoon

For Angie and Jim the honeymoon was definitely an afterthought in their budget, but that didn't stop them creating a unique honeymoon. 'We'd simply run out of cash and with a new home to furnish we thought we should postpone the grand world trip,' says Jim. Undaunted, they set about using their two weeks to do something different. 'We've always loved France so we thought we could go touring,' says Angie. 'My friend offered to lend me her ancient Camper van so once we'd sorted the insurance and a service, we had very few expenses to cover.' In their battered mobile home they crossed to France, got out the maps and headed south on the back roads. 'In the end we only got to half the places we'd planned,' adds Jim. 'It was a leisurely and relaxing road trip with plenty of good food and wine every evening. We count it as our best holiday ever.'

WHILE YOU ARE AWAY

After the party comes the clearing up – but the good news is that you can delegate like mad since many of the jobs need to be sorted in your absence. Here are things you might need to consider.

- **Final payments** Any outstanding bills should have been settled on or immediately after your wedding day. The only exception is disputed bills or undelivered goods and services. Put family or friends onto the case and ask them to tie up loose ends for you.
- **Return of glasses/alcohol** Glasses and sale-or-return alcohol needs to be returned to the store so the refund can be organised. Remember that glasses need to be washed and counted and that someone should also make a note of the number of returned bottles.
- **Wedding outfits** Anything that was hired should be returned as soon as possible. Hire companies accept a certain amount of wear and tear, but not great rips in sleeves or non-removable mud stains.
- **Dry cleaning** Your wedding dress/suit will need dry cleaning. Wedding dresses should be taken to a specialist and any tricky marks or stains (e.g. chocolate, red wine) should be pointed out. The more information they have about what caused it the better. Also remember that early dry cleaning is more likely to remove the stain. Don't attempt a DIY job as you will make things worse.
- **Anything borrowed** You may have borrowed chairs, garden furniture or tableware from friends and relatives. This needs to be returned after it has been checked for damage. You should offer to pay for any breakages.

DID YOU KNOW...? STORING YOUR DRESS SAFELY

The best way to store your dress is to wrap it in tissue paper. Make sure this is acid-free (ask for ph-neutral paper). It needs to be kept in a dry and dark place, but air it periodically and check that it doesn't get attacked by moths. A few balls of cedar wood or lavender sachets will help to protect it and keep it smelling fresh. Avoid using mothballs as the strong smell can be unpleasant and will linger in the fabric.

THE PERFECT THANK-YOU

There is one last duty you have to perform – and that is to write some thank you notes. This may seem an awesome task if you have hundreds of gifts from armies of friends and family, but a brief and personal note will cover most situations. Here are the ground rules.

What's the time limit?

Everyone is pretty understanding about thank you letters, but you should aim to get them written and in the post within two months. Leave it much longer and you will just have to write a much longer (and guilt-ridden) letter. Emails are not acceptable unless you are on an extended world trip with no access to a reliable post office, since they suggest you are too mean to buy writing paper and a stamp.

Can I type them?

An unforgivable gaffe since this suggests that you have a one-size-fits-all letter stored on your computer. A handwritten note shows that you have put personal thought into your letter, just as your guests did with your presents. If you like you can type address labels though.

So what should I write?

There is no tried-and-trusted formula here, since the letter comes from you and expresses your sentiments. There are three useful tips though. The first is to make it personal by mentioning the gift and what it will be used for. The second is to say how much you enjoyed your day and how happy you were to see them among your guests. The third is to keep the note brief – one side of notepaper will do admirably.

What if it's a cheque/cash?

This is a non-specific present, but the giver would probably like to know what you are going to spend the money on. You don't have to be too detailed, particularly if the money is going into a pot, but if you are working on your home or garden or saving up for something then express your thanks for their help with that. Everyone likes to feel his or her contribution has been useful.

CHOOSE THE RIGHT PAPER

The trick to writing a brief thank you note is to choose the right paper. Sounds obvious, but if you buy A4 writing paper you will feel obliged to write reams or your note will be stranded in a sea of white. If you go for a more diminutive size such as Duke, you can keep your note short without it looking like you've run out of steam. If you prefer a bit more colour, buy thank you cards for your guests and then write a short personal note on the left hand side.

NICE GIFT, BUT WHO'S IT FROM?

This is something you have done your best to avoid but if a gift tag has become separated from its parcel or a guest forgot to label their present in the first place, you have a much harder task writing a personal note. First, try to find out what they brought you. This detective work is best done discreetly by friends or family members, perhaps by asking around to see who bought the green vase that looks so lovely on your mantelpiece. Or they could mention their own gift in conversation and then say casually 'what did you buy for them?'. If this doesn't work then your only recourse is to write a non-specific letter thanking them for their gift and then talking about how nice it was to see them. Not a perfect solution but an acceptable one under the circumstances.

✧ SAMPLE THANK-YOU LETTERS

Here are a few short samples to get you started. Use them for guidance but don't feel you have to stick to this formula or keep them this brief, it really does depend on your own letter writing style and the relationship you have to the person receiving the letter.

LETTER 1: TO AN AUNT YOU KNOW WELL

> Dear Auntie Nancy,
>
>   Thank you so much for the lovely _____ (insert present description here). It was a real treat to return home from honeymoon and have so many presents to unwrap and your _____ looks perfect _____ (on mantelpiece/with curtains/at end of garden or other appropriate phrase).
>
>   We hope you enjoyed the wedding as much as we did. It was a real pleasure to have all our family and friends together.
>
>   It's back to reality now, but we're enjoying married life very much and hope to hold another party as soon as we've recovered from the last one!
>
>   All our love,

LETTER 2: TO FRIENDS YOU KNOW VERY WELL

> Dear George and Lucy,
>
>   It was great to see you at the wedding – thank you so much for making such a long journey with the kids in tow.
>
>   We were delighted with the cheque. You've seen the state of our garden so you know we can put the money to very good use indeed.
>
>   Hope you enjoyed yourselves as much as we did – we noticed from the wedding video that Jamie and Charlotte were covered in chocolate profiterole so at least dessert hit the mark with some of our guests!
>
>   See you soon and thanks again for the generous cheque.
>   Love,

LETTER 3: TO ABSENT DISTANT FAMILY FRIEND

Dear Mr Taylor,

Thank you so much for your card and gift of _____ (insert present description here). It was very kind of you to think of us on our wedding day and we were so sorry you couldn't celebrate with us.

It was a wonderful day – although it passed in a flash for both of us – and we couldn't have wished for better weather.

We do hope to see you again soon and thank you once again for your thoughtful gift.

Kind regards,

CREDIT WHERE IT'S DUE

There is no obligation to write and thank your wedding suppliers, but if you feel the caterer went the extra mile or were particularly pleased with the flowers then it is a nice gesture to write and let the people responsible know. Some of your comments may even be used as testimonials, which is a good way of letting other prospective brides and grooms know that they are onto a winner. Once again the letters can be brief and personal – do single out anyone who was particularly helpful or kind on the day.

ON YOUR RETURN

There can be a real sense of anti climax once you return from your honeymoon. Here are some ways to make the party mood go on for a little longer:

- **Organise a photo night** There must be hundreds of images of the party recorded on film so get a group of friends round so you can see their pictures and they can admire your wedding and holiday snaps.
- **Have a reunion** Organise a 'rematch' with your wedding crew – both as a way of saying thank you and as a chance to share some memories of the day itself. Invite the best man, ushers, chief

bridesmaid and anyone else who made the day special to a bar or restaurant. Don't foot the bill though – everyone will expect to go Dutch after the money you have spent.

- **Call in the gift list** Your Christmases have come all at once when the van turns up with goodies from your wedding. It's a chance to unwrap all the parcels and boxes and marvel at the prospect of finally having those 12 matching wineglasses and Egyptian cotton bathrobe.
- **Plan your next holiday** Planning a trip is a good way to focus on the future and give yourselves something to look forward to. Even if the holiday is a year or more away, it doesn't hurt to start thinking.

True life stories: We hosted a memory night

Returning from honeymoon can be a sobering experience – not only is the glamorous party well and truly over, but you have to settle back into the same old routine of job, housework and grocery shopping. And you are no longer the centre of attention. Aidan and Louise decided to make their homecoming special by organising a 'meet' for all their stag and hen night crew in a local restaurant a week after their return from honeymoon. 'It was a lot more restrained than the pre-wedding party, which is probably a good thing, but it was a great chance for everyone to catch up and swap stories,' says Aidan. 'We had tans and felt rested after our two-week break so it gave us one chance to enter the room like the bride and groom,' adds Louise.

USEFUL SOURCES

Time to get started on planning your wedding. Listed here are sources of essential wedding information and advice plus suppliers of everything from stag weekends to confetti. Happy hunting!

CIVIL CEREMONIES

British Humanist Society   www.humanism.org.uk

General Register Office   www.gro.gov.uk

General Register Office for Scotland   www.gro-scotland.gov.uk

General Register Office for Northern Ireland   www.groni.gov.uk

General Register Office for Ireland   www.groireland.ie

RELIGIOUS CEREMONIES

Church of England and Wales   www.cofe.anglican.org

Church of Scotland   www.churchofscotland.org.uk

Church of Ireland   www.ireland.anglican.org

Catholic Church   www.catholic-church.org.uk

Baptist Union   www.baptist.org.uk

Jewish Marriage Council   www.jmc-uk.org

Methodist Church   www.methodist.org.uk

Religious Society of Friends (Quakers)   www.quaker.org.uk

United Reformed Church   www.urc.org.uk

INTERFAITH ADVICE

2-in-2-1   www.2-in-2-1.co.uk

Inter Faith Marriage Network   www.interfaithmarriage.org.uk

NAME CHANGING

UK Deed Poll Service   www.ukdps.co.uk

UK Identity and Passport Service   www.ukpa.gov.uk

Irish Deed Poll (Courts Service)   www.courts.ie

Irish Passport Service (Department of Foreign Affairs)
www.foreignaffairs.gov.ie

LOCAL AND NATIONAL WEDDING SUPPLIERS

Confetti   www.confetti.co.uk

WeddingGuideUK   www.weddingguideuk.com

The Wedding Guide   www.theweddingguide.co.uk

WEDDING SHOWS

The Designer Wedding Show   www.designerweddingshow.co.uk

National Wedding Show   www.nationalweddingshow.co.uk

UK Wedding Shows   www.theukweddingshows.co.uk

ENGAGEMENT AND WEDDING RINGS

British Jewellers' Association   www.bja.org.uk

Crafts Council   www.craftscouncil.org.uk

De Beers   www.debeers.com

OUTFIT HIRE

Hire Society   www.hire-society.com

Moss Bros   www.mossbros.co.uk/hire

STATIONERY

Bride & Groom Wedding   www.brideandgroomdirect.co.uk

Special Day   www.specialdaydirect.co.uk

Wedding Stationery Gallery   www.wedding-stationery-gallery.co.uk

STAG AND HEN NIGHT PARTIES

Big Weekends   www.bigweekends.com

Hen Heaven   www.henheaven.co.uk

Last Night of Freedom   www.lastnightoffreedom.co.uk

Party Box   www.partybox.co.uk

Silly Jokes   www.sillyjokes.co.uk

Stag Weekends   www.stagweekends.co.uk

GIFT LISTS

Debenhams   www.debenhamsweddings.com

John Lewis   www.johnlewisgiftlist.com

Marks & Spencer   www.marksandspencer.com/giftregistry

Marriage Gift List   www.marriagegiftlist.com

Smart Wedding Lists   www.smartweddinglists.com

The Wedding Shop   www.weddingshop.com

Wrap It   www.wrapit.co.uk

PHOTOGRAPHY & VIDEO

Association of Professional Videomakers   www.apv.org.uk

The Master Photographers Association   www.thempa.com

Society of Wedding & Portrait Photographers   www.swpp.co.uk

Wedding Photojournalist Association   www.wpja.org

WEDDING INSURANCE

E&L Insurance   www.eandl.co.uk

Events Insurance   www.events-insurance.co.uk

Wedding Insurance   www.weddinginsurance.co.uk

Wedding Plan   www.weddingplaninsurance.co.uk

ENTERTAINERS

EntsWeb Directory   www.entsweb.co.uk

Function Junction   www.functionjunction.co.uk

The Events Company.co.uk   www.theeventscompany.co.uk

DANCE CLASSES

First Dance UK   www.firstdance.co.uk

First Wedding Dance   www.firstweddingdance.co.uk

Dance Matrix   www.dancematrix.com

SOURCES FOR SPEECHES

Famous Quotes   www.famousquotes.me.uk

Quotez   www.quotations.co.uk

Comedy Zone   www.comedy-zone.net

INDEX